"In this long-awaited labor of love, Karl Tra[...] by the hand and shows them the very natu[...] vis explores the generosity of God, generosi[...] finally, generosity with God, ultimately making the case for how giving from a posture of gratitude can transform the giver's life. The journey described is a gift for all who desire to walk more closely with our generous and loving God."
—Kristine Miller, partner and executive vice president, Horizons Stewardship

"Karl Travis is the perfect pastor to write a book on stewardship, because he genuinely treats all of life as a gift. And he does so because he wholeheartedly believes and trusts in God's goodness, abundance, and graciousness. This book reframes generosity in a robustly theological way, mirroring the generous heart of God. Expect to be inspired and moved toward opening your hands and heart."
—Danielle Shroyer, author, speaker, spiritual director

"Holy cow! If you think, as I thought, that you pretty much understand Christian stewardship and generosity, read this book. You will quickly feel embarrassed, as I did, over your prior conceits. And your grasp of God's generosity will transform yours, which in turn will transform that of those you influence. Karl Travis and his book are gifts of that divine generosity for us all to treasure and share."
—Jack Haberer, pastor, author, former editor and publisher of *The Presbyterian Outlook*

"Karl Travis sees with the eye of a perceptive pastor, writes with the verve of a joyous companion, and argues with the existential urgency of a dying man. This is a book bursting with faith, hope, and love, convincing us that God has given us everything we need; but it is also a manual of practical wisdom, contending that generosity is the best investment. Reading this book won't just make you a more effective pastor; it will make you a more profound human being."
—Samuel Wells, author and vicar, St. Martin-in-the-Fields

"If you are looking for a simple how-to manual on conducting a stewardship campaign, you need to keep looking. But if you are looking for an intriguing and in-depth study in generosity and how to bring a congregation along on the journey, you will find it in Karl Travis's new book, *God's Gift of Generosity: Gratitude beyond Stewardship*. Travis takes the reader through a personal and thorough dive into the theology of stewardship, starting with God's generosity. He also handles thorny stewardship dilemmas, including tithing. Pointing to numerous biblical references and intimate stories, he guides us through rethinking tithing.

Many have come to believe that tithing is passé and no longer understood among today's congregations, and thus it should be abandoned. Travis makes the case that if we truly understand God's generosity, the idea of tithing will come naturally. The book encourages the congregation, pastor, and church leadership to spend valuable time studying the depth of God's generosity in order to launch a new methodology of stewardship.

I have had the honor and privilege of walking with Travis through the last decade and have witnessed him exhibit generosity of soul, spirit, and love through a journey that would have made Job quake. His staring death in the imminent face and keeping faith through it all was the most magnificent example of who and what we are called to be.

This book will rock your world in a good way. It is written with humility, humor, and passion. May you be blessed as I was."
—Rick Young, president, Texas Presbyterian Foundation

"Karl Travis's themes of gratitude and generosity crackle with profound examples that remind us in this often-dispirited time that, at its essence, the church is still alive and hopeful. At its very heart, this book beckons us to practice boldly an unafraid discipleship grounded by the keystone of consistent generosity and religious joy. This book is not simply a primer for stewardship committees. More profoundly, it is an invitation to explore the landscape of a deeper faith. Those who love this faith and those who wish to love it more will be blessed by the wisdom within these pages."
—Ted Wardlaw, president emeritus, Austin Presbyterian Theological Seminary

GOD'S GIFT OF GENEROSITY

Access free resources at
www.wjkbooks.com/Generosity to expand the use
of this book to group study and worship settings.

GOD'S GIFT OF GENEROSITY

Gratitude beyond Stewardship

KARL B. TRAVIS

WESTMINSTER
JOHN KNOX PRESS
LOUISVILLE • KENTUCKY

First edition
Published by Westminster John Knox Press
Louisville, Kentucky

24 25 26 27 28 29 30 31 32 33—10 9 8 7 6 5 4 3 2 1

Scripture quotations from the New Revised Standard Version of the Bible are copyright © 1989 by the Division of Christian Education of the National Council of the Churches of Christ in the U.S.A. and are used by permission.

Excerpts from James K. Manley, "Spirit" in the *Presbyterian Hymnal* and "Spirit, Spirit of Gentleness," in *Glory to God* are reprinted by permission of the author. All rights reserved.

Book design by Erika Lundbom
Cover design by Leah Lococo

Library of Congress Cataloging-in-Publication Data

Names: Travis, Karl B., author.
Title: God's gift of generosity : gratitude beyond stewardship / Karl B.
   Travis.
Description: First edition. | Louisville : WJK, Westminster John Knox
   Press, [2024] | Summary: "Ideal for pastors who must engage in one of
   the most uncomfortable tasks of their role: asking people for money.
   This book is for the pastor who wants to engage the question of why?
   during the stewardship campaign, as opposed to just how?"-- Provided by
   publisher.
Identifiers: LCCN 2024016426 (print) | LCCN 2024016427 (ebook) | ISBN
   9780664261276 (paperback) | ISBN 9781646983841 (ebook)
Subjects: LCSH: Christian stewardship. | Generosity--Religious
   aspects--Christianity.
Classification: LCC BV772 .T69 2024 (print) | LCC BV772 (ebook) | DDC
   248/.6--dc23/eng/20240514
LC record available at https://lccn.loc.gov/2024016426
LC ebook record available at https://lccn.loc.gov/2024016427

Most Westminster John Knox Press books are available at special quantity discounts when purchased in bulk by corporations, organizations, and special-interest groups. For more information, please e-mail SpecialSales@wjkbooks.com.

Proceeds from the sale of this book will be donated to Presbyterian Disaster Assistance.

For my Parents
who gave so much from so little

And for Jaci
whose generosity is impressed across my life

CONTENTS

ACKNOWLEDGMENTS

I KNOW NOTHING EXCEPT THAT WHICH I WAS TAUGHT, SO I THINK OF this book as a collection of borrowed thoughts—but not stolen ones—a collection of borrowed thoughts resynthesized. My debts are incalculable.

My life and faith have been molded by four congregations, where I learned, worshiped, and served. I was raised within First Presbyterian Church, Tulia, Texas. As a pastor, I served three congregations: Westminster Presbyterian Church, Roswell, New Mexico; Grosse Ile Presbyterian Church, Grosse Ile, Michigan; and First Presbyterian Church, Fort Worth, Texas. To the congregations I served, you laughed when you were supposed to and didn't when you could have. We grew together. Thank you.

More parishioners have influenced and inspired me than I can name, yet several have so fed me that neglecting their names would be akin to a table grace with no mention of food: Jane Berckes, Jeff Bledsoe, Marvin and Veva Byrd, Ron and

Flora Case, John and Nancy Colina, Tim McKinney, Collin and Emily Hadley, Steve Hudgens, Phil and Jeanne Kennedy, Matt Mildren, Herd Midkiff, John Mitchell, Helen Morrison, Fred Oberkircher, Sue Quinn, and Vernon Rew.

God has gifted me with remarkable colleagues, among them Mark Denton, Dana Fickling, Jan Holmes, Robyn Michalove, Kristine Miller, Amy Parker, Mark Peake, Doug Scott, Josh Stewart, Mike Thompson, Rick Young, Michael Waschevski, and Shannon Webster. Their personal faith and professional practices of generosity have given me hope and inspiration.

In fledgling and unformed shape, the ideas in this book have been received however gratefully by conference participants, worshiping congregations, retreat-goers, and magazine readers over the last three decades. My favorite part of writing, speaking, and preaching is listening afterward. Thank you for your critiques and insights.

I owe special thanks to Ron Case, John Colina, Doug Huneke, and Jon Nuelle for their attentive eyes and keen minds while editing drafts. Robert Ratcliff, editor-in-chief at Westminster John Knox Press, was surprisingly open to publishing this book even after an illness-induced respite of seven years. I laughed out loud when he told me that my excuse—dying— was the best excuse for an unfinished manuscript anyone had ever offered him. Bob, thanks for my relaxed deadline.

Kathi and Bill Rito, Raley Talieferro, and Wally Tate are brave and generous for allowing me to share their intensely personal stories.

Sam Wells has been since seminary a gift of inspiration, wisdom, and deep friendship. I owe Sam the rhetorical playfulness in contrasting for and with, though I have deployed it much less deftly than him.

My four siblings—Doug, Jan, Drew, and Kristi—are each church leaders and possessed of enormous generosity. This is no coincidence, of course, learning as we did from our parents Jane and Murray Travis, whose faith and liberality have influenced far more people than ever they would have acknowledged.

No one could have told me how much I would love my children nor how much I would learn from them—Audrey, Madelene, and Ian—and later, my stepchildren—Rachel and Jacob. They do not realize yet how much I owe them. Please, do not tell them.

My wife, Jaci, is a font of inspiration and support, a partner and a sounding board. Jaci saved my life—literally and figuratively. Without Jaci's insistent encouragement, this book would never have been completed. She is my partner, my coach, and my wellspring.

Since God reads our thoughts, God need not read our books, so it might seem hackneyed to acknowledge God. Yet, any book on generosity must from its first pages celebrate the Divine's lavish provision that ultimately roots and enables all subsequent generosities.

Deo gratia.

PREFACE

I WRITE THIS FROM MY DEATH BED. YOU MIGHT THINK THIS MELO-dramatic, yet it is true that I am writing from a hospital bed delivered to my house when I went on hospice care. My doctors feared a quick dying—no more than 30 days—but that was two years ago.

I was healthy when I contracted to write this book in 2014 and began writing in good faith. Then, my health failed. In a seven-year avalanche, illness swept away my energy, professional life, and mobility, but not my faith, and certainly not my gratitude. In fact, the terminal diagnosis quietly confirmed that I am truly a Christian. I had preached for 29 years, mind you, yet a terminal diagnosis has a way of proving the pudding.

After my will was finalized, we wrote my funeral service, and I finished my family's genealogy, I dusted off the manuscript to discover that what I had written about generosity seems even more relevant to me now, particularly as

COVID-19 leaves the world guessing about the future of the church, wondering if American Christians have been lulled into permanent complacency amidst the pandemic interlude. With the gross domestic product bouncing up and down like a NASCAR speedometer—and unemployment, housing evictions, and church attendance with it—how might COVID-19 impact attitudes toward giving?

My father was also a pastor, as was my father's father, and his father's father. And both brothers, also. (My brother Drew allows that this is not a credential but rather a confession.) Dad once observed sardonically that ministry has become a series of endless meetings punctuated by worship services. Amidst this disjointed, frenetic, and spirit-smudging lifestyle, most ministers seem feverishly in search of quality materials to inform and shorten preparation time. Publishers are happy to oblige, of course, which explains the torrent of beautiful and intriguing advertisements that cross every pastor's desk and email screen, ads detailing programmatic, step-by-step instructions for every variety of institutional task.

I was a pastor. That means that I was also preacher, writer, administrator, supervisor, counselor, caregiver, program planner, project manager, meeting organizer and moderator, leadership guru, and yes: a fundraiser. With so much on my professional plate, I could have been forgiven my temptation to use such packaged programs, particularly those regarding Christian stewardship. Stewardship is, after all, parish ministry's high-wire act; the risk is elevated, and everyone is watching. Any stewardship book or program is enticing if it hands pastors a ready-made vocabulary and an out-of-the-box process for the annual stewardship season.

There are a good many such books out there, too, books on how to conduct an annual stewardship campaign, books on the mechanics of motivating and inspiring parishioners to share God's bounty. Many are quite good.

And yet, as a pastor I longed for something different. The stewardship books which litter my library are not necessarily unbearably slick nor unreasonably mechanical. Rather, it seems to me, they are incomplete. My library is chock-full of helpful books describing how: how to conduct an effective annual effort, how to oversee a capital campaign, how to begin a faithful planned giving ministry. How is important.

But I wanted more. I wondered, "Why?" Why give? For a lover of God, why does generosity matter? This question is more basic and far-reaching than, "Why give to my church?" It is an expansive and bone-deep question: Why give at all, to anything, to anyone, at any time?

Secular philanthropy proffers carefully researched answers detailing why people give. Some people want tax benefits. Some want their names on a wall or in a newsletter. Some want to improve the world, to help a favored group. Some give without conscious motivation at all. Donors offer these reasons and more. But do these answers fully encompass the Christian impulse to give? Do they satisfy the disciple, one who seeks to follow the mystery of divinity? Do followers of Jesus give only for these reasons, or do people of faith act also on a qualitatively different impulse, a more overtly spiritual motive?[1]

Somewhere back in Sunday school we learned the answers to this question, why we give. We know why as well as we know the Lord's Prayer and the Twenty-third Psalm. We give to please God. We give in response to God's grace. We give because God says to. We give to grow. Then, having spat out the theological truisms, we rush to plan the stewardship season.

It's no wonder that those in our pews hear the same threadbare reasoning annually and assume that the entire endeavor has mostly to do with subscribing the church's budget. They do not hear an invitation into the generous heart of God. They do not sense a passionate summons to practice a primary spiritual discipline. They do not hear an excited call to discover a deep sense of inner and communal joy, a bidding to be enveloped by God's already vibrant and ongoing ministries of redemption and reconciliation, and all of it amidst God's larger endeavor to do nothing less than renew the world.

Surely, I thought, there must be a more intellectually satisfying, a more spiritually gratifying, a more authentically religious explanation for practiced generosity. This book seeks a deeper vision for disciplined, mindful, and joyous generosity.

I have divided its contents into roughly equal thirds. The second and third portions build upon the first. The book seeks to ask in sequence, what? Then, so what? And finally, now what?

The "what" is God—our mutuality with the divine creator, the wellspring of generosity. The "so what" is the practice of generosity in our context—early twenty-first century North America mainline Protestantism. The "now what" discusses several of the thorniest stewardship questions pastors and leaders ask about the church's stewardship practices. In theological terms, this book attempts to relish the timeless nature of God and then faithfully apply its delight in our own time and methods. It seeks to move from orthodoxy (correct doctrine) to orthopraxis (correct conduct), though in our lived experience that movement may go in either direction.

Allow me a word, too, about terms. When I was first contacted, I was asked about writing a book on stewardship. I hesitated. Stewardship, like so many religious words, has been coopted for non-religious purposes. The word has not been so much stolen as it has been massaged, manipulated, redefined. Search the website of any major oil or gas company, of most mining companies, of most major automakers for the term stewardship. Do the same with most capital investment or wealth management firms. You might be surprised by the frequent and elastic use of the word stewardship.

Taking a cue from any of several biblical parables, and particularly from the parable of the Unjust Steward, Christians have long defined stewardship as the wise management of another's property, namely, God's property. If "the earth is the LORD's and all that is in it" (Ps. 24:1), stewardship has been for us the heady task of managing God's stuff. And if the devil is in the details, here the details are about management.

British Petroleum and Fidelity Investments have retained the values of management in their use of the term stewardship, but they have plucked from God's soil the very roots of Christian values and motivations. I applaud the current concern to wed stewardship with environmental and economic sustainability, and yet the singular concentration on stewardship as management has now overwhelmed richer dimensions of the word's deepest meanings. Stewardship has become too singularly synonymous with management, and as such, has been reduced to instrumentalism, minimized to mere utilitarianism.

There is another term which implicitly carries the goals of wise management while exuding the broader and more liberal biblical concept we wish to explore. That word is generosity.[2] If stewardship's verb has become "manage," generosity's verb should be "give." Managing and giving are related, but they also are different. Stewardship and generosity are not synonyms. Though I certainly do not want to eliminate management as a part of stewardship's definition, I prefer the word generosity. If experiencing God's grace and open-handedness inspires us to some particular verb, excites us to some specific behavior, I daresay that managing is part of it, but giving is all of it.

A word about context is also in order. I write as a white male pastor who served middle and upper-middle class mainline congregations reflective of the denomination (the Presbyterian Church (U.S.A.)) to which they belong. I have tried to write a book useful to people in similar settings, though I do hope that these observations are relevant also in a broader context. If I had written a book aimed at African American pastors and parishioners in, say, Detroit, or targeted to storefront parishes of migrant workers, I would have emphasized different themes and confronted different obstacles. Since the mainline is my experience and my target, I speak from and to it. By doing so, and as wealth disparity becomes increasingly obvious and indefensible, I am not defending a denominationalism linked to class. I do not argue that such is right. I simply observe that such is real, even while lamenting the church's inability to share resources between wealthier and poorer congregations.

Finally, I rejoice in God's providence that my thoughts emerge from my biography. While I hope that what I have written is true, I celebrate also that all truth is revealed. Truth revealed to any single person emanates from God. As such, truth becomes apparent within relationships, specifically through individual families, invariably in a humanly limited context, always in a solitary lifetime. We are our stories and our stories are us. Alongside ideas about God and observations about the church, I have also shared stories and illustrations from my life, my family, and from my pastoral experience. This book is unique, then, completed in the rich, pensive, and stolen days somewhere between a terminal diagnosis and death, when contemplation is at its richest. It is an unusual fusion, part theological and biblical reflection, part pastoral and personal memoir, part cultural criticism, and part instruction manual.

For the pastor, both preaching and writing balance in the tantalizing equilibrium between "Thus sayeth the Lord" and "It seems to me." If you make it to the last page, I pray that "Thus sayeth the Lord" regarding God's generosity is at least clear enough that you will celebrate your past generosities and commit yourself to becoming ever more generous.

Karl Travis
Lent 2022

Part I

God's Generosity

H<small>E COULDN'T WAIT TO TELL ME</small>. H<small>E KNEW</small> I <small>WOULD GRIMACE</small>. H<small>E</small>
was right.

In his travels, one of my parishioners happened into a faraway congregation on the proverbial "Stewardship Sunday."
Stewardship Sunday is that once-a-year occasion to talk about
money that most churches treat like an annual flu shot—the
reluctant willingness to be poked in the body's nether regions,
hoping that it will inoculate you for the remainder of the year.
The chair of the stewardship committee stood uncomfortably
in the chancel, hands in his pockets, his feet shuffling like an
eighth grader at his first dance.

"I hate this as much as you do," he began, "talking about
money. But we must. The staff hasn't had a raise in four years,"
he droned on, "and the air conditioner has gotten old. There
is a leak in the sanctuary roof. I know that you don't want to
hear this, and I don't really want to say it, but the church needs
more money. So please, give more."

He sat down much more quickly than he had stood up.
There had been no mention of the church's ministries beyond
its walls, no calling to mind of the church's role in the world,
no allusion to past faithfulness, and no reference to future
vision. That volunteer chairperson spoke of the church but
not of the believer, talked about the congregation's need to
receive but not the disciple's need to give.

And, if all of this was not deadening enough, he made no
mention of God.

How many times are similar lectures offered every autumn?
My hunch is that across America, otherwise faithful and well-
intentioned pastors and parishioners stand before their fellow
disciples not much wanting to, not knowing what they should
say. They follow the same threadbare reasoning and make the
theological pitch we are most accustomed to: stewardship is
about the church's need, the church's mission, the church's
budget. There isn't much mention of the individual. Worse

yet, if God is mentioned at all, references to God have more to do with guilt and obligation than with joy and generosity.

Have we been doing the wrong thing really well?

Let us reverse the conversation. Let us begin with God.

I've heard it said that American Protestants are Calvinists whether they know it or not. Calvin was the brilliant sixteenth-century theologian who, while only in his twenties, penned his Institutes of the Christian Religion. He began the two-volume tome by telling us that our faith may begin at one of two starting points—with us, or with God. And yet, if we seek self-understanding, it seems best to begin by contemplating God. To better see ourselves, first we contemplate the face of God or, perhaps more poetically, the heart of God, the unimaginably generous heart of God. If our question is, then, "Why are we to give?" our search begins with God, in God. Human generosity finds both its seed and its harvest in God's generosity.

Chapter 1

THE GENEROSITY *OF* GOD

"God so loved the world that God gave…"

—John 3.16

GOD'S FIRST GENEROSITIES

THE BIBLE TELLS THE STORY OF GOD'S BURNING DESIRE FOR RELA-
tionship, for restoration, for redemption. The trajectory of
this narrative is so assumed, so implicit to our understanding
of God's story, that we must pause even to remember that it
was the ancient Jews who invented time, or at least our understanding of it.[1] Before ancient Israel, people thought of time
as a circle, the rhythmic order of events happening in cycles,
and as such, time was going nowhere in particular. Life was
just one thing after another, and then you died.

Ancient Jews, however, heard and sensed God intervening
in the world. What is more, they understood God to be taking
humanity and history somewhere. They stretched history from
a circle into a line, a straight line, a story with a beginning, a
middle, and an end. Among the Hebrews' greatest contributions to civilization, then, is the striking reality that God is

present in the world, that God is taking the world from something to something else, and that a nation's shared life—and an individual's life—can therefore have meaning. Humanity is capable of participating in God's movement and meaning, a story which has a beginning, a middle, and an end.

The Bible, then, is the compiled drama of God's love for God's people, for all of humankind, and for all God's creation. It is a collection of stories, a narrative of successive accounts describing God's interactions with people across time, a story with meaning, purpose, and direction. Thus, the stories contained in this holy book are commonly summarized something like this: God creates, then humanity falls, then God forgives, then God redeems, and finally, in the future, God completes the plan. Our story with God is one of creation, relationship, and then redemption, reconciliation, restoration, and ultimately joyous generosity. This describes, in general, the Bible's trajectory.

And yet, might there be an additional summary, a complementary interpretation that connects the entirety of God's story to our understanding of Christian generosity? Is the arc of creation, fall, redemption, completion the only way to comprehend the Bible? I have come to believe in my bones that the biblical story outlines the contours of God's nature, and that God's nature is emphatically, eternally, and passionately generous, forever seeking creative relationship with us and the cosmos.

No one worships a stingy God. If "God loves a cheerful giver" (2 Cor. 9:7), humanity loves a generous God.

People are drawn to God by dramatically different characteristics. Yet no matter how else we relish the divine, generosity is God's universally appreciated quality. For some, God is above all things loving. For others, God is first forgiving. Some are drawn to a God who is just, or merciful, or gracious. No matter your preferred divine quality—loving, forgiving, wise, just, powerful, merciful, creative—what finally evokes your passion is how generously God shares it. God gave, God gives, God promises to give yet more. Generosity more than describes what God does. Generosity describes who God is. Before and after God is anything else, God is generous.

Someone said that there are only two prayers: *please* and *thank you. Please* precedes God's generosity. *Thank you* is our response to God's generosity.

The entire Bible may be framed as the epic story of God's generosity. Since the Bible details God's generous nature, it opens with a story of generosity, with God creating the world and sharing it with human beings, God's chosen image upon the earth. After God created humankind in his image, "God blessed them, and God said to them, ... 'I have given you every plant yielding seed'" (Gen. 1:28–29). God continues. The gifts include all green things, trees and their fruits, too. Adam, Eve, and their descendants are lavishly provisioned.

Though well beyond our scope here, it's nonetheless interesting to read a prescientific explanation of creation which already intuits the insanely lavish, bountiful, dynamic, and incredibly complex biosphere that human beings have found awaiting our exploration. From our cells to the skies, the matrix of life is tantalizing evidence of God's creative generosity.

Following the flood, in a moment of expansive mercy and overwhelming hope, God's disappointment receding with the waters, God surprisingly says to Noah, "just as I gave you the green plants, I give you everything" (Gen. 9:3b). Everything. If Adam and Eve received all green things, the plants and trees and produce, God's generosity now grows to include "every bird of the air, everything that creeps on the earth" (Gen. 1:30). God's generosity is in measure with God's mercy. We expect that humanity's faithlessness will discourage God's generosity. Nonetheless, from destruction comes a second chance. Human failure and folly draw from God ever greater generosity. Now, the human family receives every blessing the earth is capable to provide.

The story continues. God chooses, calls, and makes covenant with Abraham and Sarah. God gives them blessing, promising them descendants as there are stars in the sky and grains
of sand. The surprises begin with an unexpected son born late
in life, named in joyous gratitude Isaac, "He will laugh."

Next God gives to Isaac and Rebekah—likewise late and
against biological odds—twin boys, Jacob and Esau. In surprising and almost comical fashion, the covenant generously
continues.

Next God gives to Jacob and his several wives many sons,
from which come the tribes of Israel. Joseph is among them,
of course, to whom God gives protection in Joseph's strange
sojourn into service in the pharaoh's court. Even in Egyptian
exile, even away from home, God's gifts abound. Despite a
drought, because of the drought, God reunites Jacob's family
under Joseph's protection in faraway Egypt. In the space of a
generation, however, God's people slide from freedom toward
bondage and slavery.

In a retelling of Joseph's story, Walter Brueggemann has
shaped a generation of stewardship preachers. Brueggemann
reminds us of the story's deeper implications, reminds us
that the Hebrew people find themselves in foreign servitude
because they forget God's generosity, forget God's promise of
provision. Instead, they become captive to, fall prey to, Pharaoh's "myth of scarcity."[2] Forgetting the "orgy of fruitful-
ness" beginning with creation, God's people become beholden
to monopoly, captive to fear, enslaved to the doubt that God
will provide. They forget God's generosity.

God's generosity reaches a crescendo in the story of Moses.
God calls Moses to lead the people from Egyptian bondage.
In their exodus—the paradigmatic event of the entire Old
Testament story—God showers his people with two gifts. In
one version of his now classic hymn "Spirit," James Manley
describes the movement this way:

You swept through the desert, you stung with the sand,
And you gifted your people with a law and a land.[3]

God "gifts" God's people with commandments—for the community's safety—and with a home—for the community's prosperity. The Ten Commandments and the promised land join the list of God's generous gifts for God's people.

There is another version of "Spirit," a variant with a distinct and fascinating difference.

"You swept through the desert, you stung with the sand,
And you goaded your people with a law and a land."[4]

God "gifted" his people "with a law and a land." God "goaded" his people "with a law and a land." Which is it? Both.

Gifts goad. Gifts provoke. Gifts inspire response.

For the remainder of the Old Testament, the people's fidelity to God is measured by their remembering and responding to the twin provision of commandment and homeland. Every Passover meal remembers God's gifts of flight, freedom, family, and home. Every taste of matzo and bitter herbs recalls and relishes God's generosity.

Remembering God's generosity becomes central to the people's identity and ritual. When the people remember God's generosity, they flourish. When they forget God's generosity, the people wander and stray. Moses, by now an old man, dying, chastises the people not merely for unfaithfulness. Theirs is a particular unfaithfulness, rooted in forgetfulness. They have forgotten God's generosity. "You were unmindful of the Rock that bore you; you forgot the God who gave you birth" (Deut. 32:18).

The Hebrew Scripture continues largely in this vein, God's people chastised again and again, one misfortune after another rooted in forgetting God's generosity. It is the message to King David, the greatest king of Israel, not because he is the most

powerful but because he is the most forgiven. It is the message
to King Solomon, possessed of wisdom greater than otherwise
possible. It is the message as the two kingdoms divide and fail
and fall, that the pathway back to God is found by remembering God's prior generosities, trusting them, and responding to
them. It is the message as God's people are sent into exile, all
the while hoping to return to the promised land. The importance of remembering and responding to God's generosity is
the message standing behind every prophet's wagging finger
and clenched fist.

The point is clear. Remembering God's generosity inspires
God's people to trust and faithfulness. Forgetting God's generosity brings idolatry and isolation, arrogance and exile. God
is not arbitrary or punitive, either. God's generosity is given
with no strings other than, of course, that remembering it connects the people to their creator, which connects them to their
deepest selves. Forgetting God's generosity is akin to forgetting oneself, cutting one's life at the root.

God's generosity is so central to the identity of God's people, so basic, that the foundational Hebrew sin is forgetting it.

This is the arc of God's first generosities. God gives joyously, graciously, lovingly. As God's people remember, they
remain attached to God, and they thrive. When they forget,
they lose touch with what matters most, and they wither.

Then, as the Old Testament concludes, it is as though God
has a choice to make. It is clear that God has every right to
abandon the entire project. Will God rest content with God's
prior generosities, unappreciated as it appears they have
grown? Or, will God repeat the cycle, respond to the people's
doubts by showering upon them even greater generosity?

The answer is earthshaking. As God's provision multiplies
from Eden to Noah, God will give yet more. The biblical story
is a dynamic, sequential adding on of God's good gifts, one
atop the other. It is a tale of relentless, dynamic generosity. If

one gift does not do, God will give another. Then another. The Christian story is the saga of a loving creator so compelled by love, so possessed of grace, so hungry for relationship that there seems no end to God's *willingness* to give.

And, there is no limit to God's *capacity* to give. Until, that is, God gives all that God has.

We have arrived at the essence of the Christian faith. In the center of time, at the turning point for all meaning, God gives yet again. This time, God's generosity knows no constraints. It is limitless and expansive, extravagant, and reckless. This time, God gives God's very self. If God's generosity in creation and covenant, in commandment and the promised land, have not yet convinced us of the heart of the matter, God will amplify and complete all of it with even greater generosity. Now, God gives God's own child, Jesus.

GOD'S CENTRAL GENEROSITY

It is perhaps the most memorized biblical passage. People glue it to bumpers, stick it on refrigerators, and scribble it across posters for display at football and basketball games. "For God so loved the world that he gave his only Son, so that everyone who believes in him may not perish but may have eternal life." (John 3:16).

What sticks with people, apparently, comes in the second half of the proclamation. It has to do with believing and having, it has to do with everlasting life. This is our culture's dominant focus, the part about our eternal life with God. God's only son came and lived and laughed and taught and died and rose again, and because of that, we may be ushered into eternity. As Huston Smith notes, Christianity's staying power comes from its dealing with the chief dilemmas of human existence, the anxiety of our guilt and the fear of our death.[5] This is indescribably good news. God has dealt with what haunts us most deeply, what plagues us more powerfully. We cannot repair what most ails us, so God does. Only God can. We will not perish but we will have everlasting life.

We love this message, the second half of John's proclamation. We are like children on Christmas morning, rushing to the tree, ripping the wrapping from our packages, delighting in our gifts. Oh, kids might offer an obligatory over-the-shoulder-glance, a cursory thank-you. Thanks, Mom. Thanks, Dad. Then it is back to the gift, time to play, with little thought about the giver's motives, the giver's values, the giver's identity. Parents are rarely offended by the Christmas inattention, of course. Parents delight in their children's delight. That is what parents do. Like kids on Christmas morning, we are so excited by the gift of eternal life that we are wont to neglect the giver.

It is easy to be childlike when reading John's proclamation, easy to rush to the not perishing part, to hurry to the bit about eternal life. But biblically, something comes first. "God so loved the world that he gave." Gave. God gave.

If the Hebrew Scriptures are in essence a narrative about God's generosity, perhaps the whole of the New Testament, and certainly John's proclamation on our refrigerator doors, is a continuation of the theme. In fact, list God's gifts in a litany of thanksgiving and we might well conclude that *give* is the Bible's most significant verb.

God so loved the world that God *gave*. What is striking, what is moving, what is here transformational is the link between generosity and love. God so loved the world that God gave. The cliché has it that love is less a noun than a verb, less a thing than an action. Love unexpressed, unrevealed, untended is something less than love. Generosity, then, is what love does. Love gives. Love does not take. Love articulates itself in giving.

Notice here the Trinitarian movement of God's generosities as each person of the Godhead contributes.

God so loved that God made the world, created the cosmos—planets and plankton, stars and starfish, rocks and hills and oceans.

God so loved the world that God chose to place God's very image upon the earth's surface—human beings.

God so loved the world that God gave a promise to a particular family always to be their God, and to bless all families upon the earth through them.

God so loved the world that God sent prophets to God's people, again and again, prodding them to consciousness and righteousness, inciting their instinct for justice, beckoning them back.

God so loved the world that God gave God's only son. When the world was itself no longer enough, when God's gifts of prophets and land and law had not yet won the hearts and the trust of God's people, then, well, God gave even more. God gave of God's very self, gave a part of God's inner being. "God so loved the world that he gave his only son."

God so loved the world that God gave Jesus the courage to confront injustice and corrupt, misguided religion.

God so loved the world that God gave Jesus the passion to speak truth to power.

God so loved the world that God gave Jesus the freedom to give, to give even himself, and, crucially, the freedom not to.

Jesus so loved the world that Jesus chose utter faithfulness, chose never to compromise his identity, never to deny his experience of the Father's love. And it got him killed.

Have you ever loved someone so deeply that you were willing to put your very life in their hands? What would you have done, have thought, have felt, if they betrayed you?

This happened to God. God placed God's very self in the hands of imperial power. Torture and crucifixion followed, then death and burial. Jesus gives "his life a ransom for many" (Mark 10:45).

Next, just as we conclude that any rational God would be finished with the entire endeavor, when we reason that if love spurned is rightly withdrawn, God so loved the world that God gives yet more, even more, ever more, always more: resurrection, redemption, forgiveness, another chance, eternity.

God gave.

The New Testament story continues ceaselessly, joyfully, gladly with God's generosities. God gives the presence of the resurrected Christ. God gives the helper, the comforter, the Spirit. God gives the church. God gives the church's growth.

Framing the biblical story as a narrative of generosity comes as news to no one. That God is giving is as pedestrian an observation as saying that God is loving. It is obvious. Clear. Almost a truism. Yet, the most obvious realities are often those that most need noting precisely because in their general acceptance, they are overlooked, and in their being overlooked, their implications are neglected. It might seem apparent that before exploring our generosity we should contemplate God's. But, truth told, most of us skip right over the obvious. Most churches do. Most sermons on stewardship and generosity do. How many annual stewardship campaigns begin with the pitiful cry to subscribe to the church's budget, to repair the church's air conditioner, to fund the church's mission, with nary a mention of God?

We neglect to mention God's generosity. Or worse, we do not trust it. If so, might our distrust be the natural consequence of our making little conscious effort to recall such generosity to its fullest depth, startling frequency, or ubiquitous continuity?

Imagine a religious community that begins its stewardship conversations not with next year's budget, and not even with an inspiring vision of the individual's need to give, but rather with an exuberant and biblical picture of the generosity of God. Imagine a pastor, dreamy-eyed and visionary, standing tall and straight, speaking convincingly, and personally, and biblically, about the pervasive, decadent, ubiquitous generosity of God. Is it possible to re-root our generosity in the soil of its planter, in the field of the kingdom[6] of God?

RE-ROOTING OUR MOTIVATIONS

How often are you asked to contribute money? Think about the advertisements, the emails, the junk mail that craves your attention, which begs to inspire your generosity. If you are like me, you receive hundreds of solicitations every year, some of it on billboards and in magazines, and much of it personalized and meant especially for you.

If the solicitation comes from the not-for-profit world, and all too often from the ecclesial world, it inevitably shares one common characteristic: it pulls at our heartstrings. Photos show ramshackle huts in desperate need of repair, or flies swarming the face of a bloated child, or dogs languishing behind the wire fence of an animal shelter. The images are intended to evoke. The messages create emotional connection as a strategy to inspire.

Every not-for-profit in the secular sphere competes for our dollars by reminding us of the amazing things they will do with our money. Their assumption seems to be that first we care, then we share. If the Susan G. Komen Foundation, if the American Cancer Society, if our alumni associations can impress us with the work they do, then we might write a check. Care, then share. It is the organizational assumption of every fundraising organization in the land.

And it works. I can hardly walk into a Habitat for Humanity home without reaching for my checkbook. Likewise, every time I hear some bright-eyed 19-year-old speak about getting to go to college against the financial odds, I long to start another scholarship fund. Care, then share. So, no matter the manipulative gist of the pitch, never mind the scheming method, I must be made to care.

Sometimes the plea is not pictorial. Often it is verbal, as in a National Public Radio solicitation that reminds me that listening while not pledging is nothing short of freeloading. Unless I want to be a mooch, I will immediately pick up the phone and pledge.

Either way, the presumption is that caring precedes sharing, that first the heart longs to give and only then the hand responds.

What if this is not the only sequence of generosity? What if spiritually and biblically, Jesus suggests the exact opposite?

Matthew's sixth chapter makes a stunning claim. Jesus is teaching. "Whenever you give alms," he begins, "do not sound a trumpet before you, as the hypocrites do." He continues with counsel on praying and on fasting (Matt. 6:2–7). Jesus is coaching us on doing the right things and for the right reasons, with a purity of heart. What fascinates me is Jesus' ordering of the tripod of Jewish piety—almsgiving, praying, and fasting. Jesus begins with almsgiving. Only then does he proceed to praying and fasting. Almsgiving precedes the other disciplines of piety. Almsgiving is where we begin the religious life. Common to the three, we are not to seek notice, not to engage these disciplines because we want to draw attention to ourselves. Adulation is not our goal.

Then, at the end of the passage—after his teaching on how to pray—Jesus returns to the subject of material goods (Matt. 6:19–21). We are not to store them up, not to hoard them. After all, moth and rust consume, and thieves break in and steal. "Store up for yourselves treasures in heaven" (v. 20).

With almsgiving the starting point of piety, Jesus sums up the teaching with perhaps his most startling generosity observation of them all. "Where your treasure is, there your heart will be also" (v. 21).

If the secular philanthropic world tells us that first we must care, and only then we will share, Jesus offers a contrarian word. He says, first we share, and then we care. Treasure first. Our hearts follow our dollars and not the other way around.

When I was a teenager, I told my father that I wanted a car. He said, "Great. Get a job and buy one." So I did. I got a job, but somewhere along the way I decided not to spend my earnings on an automobile. I saved instead for college. To this day I appreciate my college degree all the more because I helped pay for it. If we want to care about something, it helps to invest ourselves in it, to contribute to its cost. Hearts follow dollars. Dollars escort hearts.

This is our clue, the smoking gun evidence that God has gifted Christian stewards with a countercultural motivation for being generous. We will return to this idea in part 2, where it reminds us of the power of being disciplined in our giving. For the moment, this truth serves well to remind us that our generosity is rooted in God's generosity. Sending money to feed starving African children is a good thing to do. Doing so brings us joy and satisfaction. There is nonetheless an even greater joy than any emotional connection we may make with the beneficiaries of our giving. After we celebrate helping hungry kids we are driven to our knees in thanksgiving, grateful that we have from God the resources to share in the first place. Our giving connects us to others. Better yet, it connects us to God.

God gives. We respond.

God initiates. We reply.

God acts. We react.

Given this sequence—that God acts first—one single word, one specific posture best describes our response to the generosity of God: gratitude.

Appreciating God's generosity, seeing it and naming it and relishing it, leads to our life-giving reply: gratitude. Gratitude is the seed of all religious trust, the soul's single most powerful tool for reorientation. Gratitude is the capacity to embrace all that surrounds us without the ego-driven insistence that we have earned it, that we deserve it, that it is ours. (Reader be warned: the human proclivity for taking credit has poisoned the spiritual growth of many a "self-made" person.)

The old adage has it that there are no atheists in foxholes. I say that there are no atheists at the Thanksgiving dinner table. To bow one's head in thanksgiving and gratitude, no matter the depth or intensity of one's religious faith—or lack of it—is implicitly to acknowledge that life's blessings come from Another. To bow one's head and say thank you, even if it is but a mutter, a mumbling and hesitant word, is to stare at the sky in wonder and give thanks for the unmerited, unearned goodness of life and all of its awe-inspiring blessings.

Visit a friend in the hospital. In my experience very personally and as a pastor, patients who improve share two habits. First, they keep their ailments in perspective by remembering that somewhere, someone has it worse. With even the direst of diagnoses, wise patients display empathy for those whose illnesses are even more challenging.

Second, they are grateful. The mastectomy patient gives thanks that the cancer has not spread to the lymph nodes. The breast cancer patient whose cancer has metastasized gives thanks that chemotherapy is available. The chemotherapy patient gives thanks for stylish wigs which adorn her now bald head. And so on. Finding cause for gratitude is redemptive because gratitude connects us to the source of all blessing, links us to the divine. Gratitude is this important. Gratitude is this powerful. Gratitude is the primal spiritual response that joins us to God's generous heart.

Martin Rinkart penned one of the church's great hymns, *Now Thank We All Our God*. Tradition has it that Rinkart was the only remaining pastor, of the original four, in Eisleben, Germany, where he served during the Thirty Years War and a severe plague in 1637 known as the Great Plague. He is said to have conducted over 4,000 funerals that year, including that of his wife. Yet, Rinkart could proclaim in his table prayer,

> Now thank we all our God with heart and hands and voices,
> who wondrous things has done, in whom this world rejoices;
> Who from our mothers' arms has blessed us on our way
> with countless gifts of love, and still is ours today.[7]

Corrie ten Boom's classic story of Christian altruism and Nazi imprisonment, *The Hiding Place*, was among the first books I read as a child. I can never forget the counsel of ten Boom's older sister when directing Corrie to give thanks for the fleas infesting the straw on their beds. Because of fleas, the German guards would not enter the room, and their absence made it possible to openly worship God.[8]

If faithful disciples have found cause for thanksgiving amidst such difficulty and deprivation, how much more powerful might gratitude be among people blessed by abundance and prosperity?

God gives. God's generosity moves us to gratitude. If the Bible records the sequence of God's generosity, if remembering and celebrating God's generosity makes us grateful, we are primed now to move from orthodoxy to orthopraxis, move from "correct thinking" to "correct conduct," from ideas to ethics.

What, then, are we to do? What does faithfulness look like? As we consider our lives, what difference might God's generosity make?

Chapter 2

GENEROSITY *FOR* GOD

"When you have finished paying all the tithe of your produce in the third year (which is the year of the tithe), giving it to the Levites, the aliens, the orphans, and the widows, so that they may eat their fill within your towns, then you shall say before the LORD your God, 'I have removed the sacred portion from the house, and I have given it to the Levites, the resident aliens, the orphans, and the widows, in accordance with your entire commandment that you commanded me; I have neither transgressed nor forgotten any of your commandments"

—Deuteronomy 26:12–13

IT IS THE OLDEST STEWARDSHIP ILLUSTRATION OF THEM ALL, PER-formed in children's sermons atop chancels across the country every autumn. I have used it myself. It reveals an important if elementary understanding of why we give. The children gather. The pastor produces a grocery sack from which she counts ten apples. Then, plucking one apple away, she teaches the children that we are to return one apple to God. The one apple belongs to God. It is God's apple. The Bible says so. The one apple is called a tithe. Giving that tithe, or tenth, is rooted in God's command to the Israelites to share a tenth of their harvest, a tenth of the best, a tenth off the top.

It was such a startling synopsis that I still remember where I was standing when an adult in a congregation where I was serving summed up the apple illustration. He had absorbed that children's sermon, internalized it, and he practiced it. "What a generous God," he exclaimed, "who lets me keep ninety percent for myself."

What a generous God indeed! Many people who tithe believe the same thing, as do many people who aspire to tithe. We are to give because God says so, and in exchange, we keep what remains. It is ours. To this way of thinking generosity is our response to God, something we do for God. We are God's instruments, God's tools. As God has shared with us, we are to share with others on God's behalf. God commands our generosity. Generosity is our obedience.

This assumption is wrapped within our traditional liturgical language. After we have gathered around the Word, after we have heard the Word read and proclaimed, finally, joyfully, we respond to the Word. We do so in prayer and with our offerings. At this high liturgical moment, we return to God "God's Tithes and Our Offerings." The message is clear. The tithe already belongs to God. Generosity beyond the tithe comes out of what is ours, and we may choose—or choose not—to share from what is ours. Give to God what rightly belongs to God.

There is much to be said for this motivation. Historically it has produced tremendous charity, motivated remarkable sacrificial sharing. Particularly for older church members, being generous for God is simply part of the religious formula. We give because we are supposed to. If Christ has no hands and no feet but our hands and our feet, Christ likewise has no pocketbook but ours. Being generous for God is a time-tested and demonstrably productive motivation for many people. If raising money is the test, this motivation bears fruit.

Being generous for God has produced, at least by outward appearances, a great many givers. It inspires a no-questions-please, simply-do-it discipline. Years ago, one of my church members, a World War II veteran, offered an interesting lesson. Long retired and drawing a monthly Social Security check, he always pledged to the church. His bank account, however, charged a fee for every check written, and, being frugal, he wanted to write only one check to the church each month. This decision brought a challenge, however. Three Sundays out of four the offering plate would pass him empty, and this was not acceptable to him. So, for the three intervening Sundays he began dropping empty offering envelopes into the plate because, he said, "I do not want an offering plate to pass me and a child see me put nothing into it."

God gives to us. We give for God. As motivations go, practicing generosity for God is certainly productive. It is obedient. It is faithful. To top it off, it is overtly biblical. A review of scripture passages concerning generosity—particularly Old Testament passages—reminds us quickly that God's people have for millennia heard God to command generosity.[1]

Nonetheless, giving for God has its limits, both functionally and theologically.

While wealthy Christians have long labelled their mammon as God's blessing, as alignment with divine favor, it's instructive to remember some recent American examples because they set the cultural stage for much of our current thinking about generosity. Consider the great American philanthropists of the early twentieth century. Note the implicit assumptions about their wealth, both its source and its meaning. Three observations are worth remembering: they understood their wealth as divine reward, they understood themselves called to distribute their wealth, and they assumed righteous wisdom in deciding how to do so.

Consider John D. Rockefeller, a man of faith who understood his wealth not merely as the result of hard work, business acumen, and good timing. It was evidence of God's blessing. There was, by the way, no small influence of social Darwinism in the psychological mix, the presumption that the best and brightest would naturally reach the top of the capitalist ladder first. Pair this presumption with an eye on providential thinking, and it is easy to see how Rockefeller could say, "I never would have been able to tithe the first million dollars I ever made if I had not tithed my first salary, which was $1.50 per week."[2] Set aside for the moment that it is actually much more difficult to tithe on a small salary than a large fortune, and that statistics show time and again that wealthy people give smaller percentages of their incomes. Notice for now Rockefeller's simple presumption that God rewards our giving by giving us more.

God gives. We give for God. The more we give, the cycle continues; God gives yet more. Here we find fertilizer for the prosperity gospel.

When Andrew Carnegie published "The Gospel of Wealth" in 1889, he was not simply bemoaning the corroded values of the children of wealth and the dangers of inherited affluence. He called upon the super wealthy to redistribute their wealth into the communities from which it had been earned. His was in many ways a laudable vision. There are still hundreds of local libraries and church organs sporting the Carnegie pedigree. With money floating up to the top, America's wealthiest men could harness a purportedly divine process to raise America's cultural standards, as they didn't stop with libraries and church organs but also built concert halls, universities, hospitals, and art collections.

Perhaps it never occurred to any of them how implicitly undemocratic the project was. No elected body voted to distribute this wealth in this way. No elected body representing the communities that received such beneficence engaged a community-needs assessment. Certainly, no elected body chose to tax its citizenry to meet these needs. One doubts also that Rockefeller or Carnegie or any in their school of philanthropy would approve of the ultimately democratic internet charity platforms, like GoFundMe.com. While few doubt the good of public libraries, the democratic question is, "Who decides?" For these uber-philanthropists, democratic process was unnecessary because they considered their wealth *prima facie* evidence that their investment decisions were in alignment with divine will. Their choices were God's choices.

For the likes of Rockefeller and Carnegie and their wannabes, wealth brought with it the presumption of divine blessing and the assumed wisdom to redistribute it righteously. Wrote Carnegie, "He is the only true reformer who is as careful and as anxious not to aid the unworthy as he is to aid the worthy, and, perhaps, even more so, for in alms-giving more injury is probably done by rewarding vice than by relieving virtue."[3] It was trickle-down theology, and it quite successfully comforted its proponents while simultaneously rationalizing the cutthroat business tactics used in wealth's accumulation.

A century later these theological assumptions thrive in American religion. One need not be a billionaire to slip toward the blessed-to-be-a-blessing model of generosity. The logic is simple and popular. God gives to me. I give for God. The reward for my giving is that God will give me more. Since by God's provision I prosper, I will respond in obedient generosity hoping all the while, however consciously, that by doing so I will also merit ever greater blessing.

In its most extreme and egregious forms, this is the essence of the prosperity gospel. Give, the teaching goes, and God will give you more, nay, tenfold! Apparently, students of the prosperity gospel do not stop to analyze that neither their impure motives nor the reality that if we give with hopes of returns, it is not giving at all. It is investing. Such logic simply incents fraudulent leadership and incites rank hypocrisy. That said, subtle traces of prosperity thinking creep their way into our psyches, into our theology, and into our pulpits. These traces are the unintended byproducts of being generous for God, and they reveal its unexplored weaknesses.

Namely, if our only or primary motive for being generous is doing so on God's behalf (and, implicitly, thereby to secure our own futures), we risk reducing our generosity to mere transaction. Like a child at the candy store, we offer our hard-earned pennies in exchange for something sweet if temporary, something savory even if it will not satisfy, at least not for long. Such is the nature of transactions. One party buys and the other sells. One participant produces and the other consumes. In exchanges, something passes hands, but nothing is changed, not really, and certainly not the parties themselves. Money changes hands, but transactions do not change hearts. Transactions leave both parties unscathed, untouched, primed only for the next transaction. Indeed, the holy grail for the now global consumer transaction business (think PayPal, Apple Pay, and Venmo) is something called the "frictionless transaction," a purchase made as quickly and anonymously as electronically possible.

How else could it be? Transformation is not the transactional goal, so it can never be the result. Transactions express the spirit of the age. This explains why Microsoft software lists the addresses and phone numbers not of family members or friends, but of "contacts." It is why Facebook can blithely label as "friends" people with whom we exchange nothing more than a click and a pic.

If we are generous simply because we are told to be, if the only reason we give is to give for God, we can be excused our error. This has been, after all, the most public teaching concerning our reasons for giving for a long time. For at least the last century, fine and faithful preachers have taken to the pulpit consumed with our institutional roles as God's salesclerks in America's religious marketplace. The church has bills to pay, after all, and mission to underwrite, and buildings to maintain, and market share to defend. And it has worked, by and large, for the good. Our churches have often been agents of righteousness, changing communities and society for the better. We have baptized the babies, said the prayers, administered the sacraments rightly. Our giving records have often been fat and healthy. Our mission budgets have affected social justice and transformation. What is more, at least some of our members have at least some of the time caught the generosity bug and discovered for themselves just how much fun it is to share God's money.

It's also apparent that our context is changing, and fast. The institutional church has been under critical assault for decades, from the outside and quite noticeably also from the inside, and that battering is quickening. Membership is declining across the denominational board. Young people increasingly identify their religious affiliation as free-floating, if they have any religious affiliation at all. (Perhaps they seek church membership as frictionless as their Facebook relationships.) In today's post-modern, post-denominational, and some say soon to be post-Christian nation, many Christians are clamoring for a deeper and more spiritual reason to grow in generosity. What has seemed a healthy and adequate rationale now feels to many somchow bare and inadequate.

Might this be true because this rationale—generosity for God—is built upon a theological model which posits an incomplete explanation of Christian faith itself?

If so, you will recognize this model instantly. It says that the chief human dilemma is sin, the single divine answer is Jesus, and the only religious goal is salvation. Salvation, mind you, is self-consciously personal, and even while my salvation might alter the way I actually live my life, still, its primary significance is guaranteeing my life with God after I die. In this model, I am a free agent, related to you only insofar as you face the same dilemma and should crave the same solution. God's love for either of us becomes operative only the moment we choose to embrace it.

In this model the biblical story is summarized something like this: God made the world beautiful and perfect and set

Adam and Eve amidst the garden, in comfort, safety, and joy. Disobedient, humanity betrayed God's intentions and introduced sin, and its greatest symptom—death—into the world. We messed up God's plans. The solution, then, since a human being messed things up, is for another human being—albeit one also divine: Jesus!—to reverse the mistake and thereby offer escape for all human beings, escape from the sin which continues to foul God's designs. Jesus has righted the ship, and we can also enjoy clear sailing, after we properly understand the storyline and embrace Jesus—properly understood—with all our heart, mind, and soul. Then and only then might our consciousness survive our heartbeat and we join God in eternity.

Here we discover the limits of this reasoning, the boundaries of the biblical story so hobbled. This is a model of God bound by if/then assumptions. God says, "If you love me, then I will save you. If you come to me, then I will embrace you. If you accept me, then I will accept you." If God's goal has only to do with our salvation, and if our salvation depends first upon our embrace of it, God's project seems strangely focused only on us, and God's love for us becomes paradoxically, uncharacteristically, strangely conditional.

It is no leap from the if/then thinking implicit in this religious trajectory to the if/then thinking of being generous for God. If God's love is conditional, our response might as well be. It is as if we say in response to God, "If you are generous to me, then I will be generous for you. If you will bless me, then I will bless the others whom you love. If you will prosper me, then I will share my resources in service to your larger project." If God is conditional, and if I am generous primarily because God has commanded me to be, then I can be conditional with my generosity. This is a quid pro quo model, a theological paradigm for you-scratch-my-back-and-I'll-scratch-yours.

Generosity rooted in this paradigm is remarkably common, frequently assumed—again, however consciously—by many American Christians. And again, it is fine so far as it goes. It produces results even if its results are implicitly unsatisfying or frustratingly temporary. I wonder, in fact, if this is why the church must conduct a full-scale generosity campaign each and every autumn, simply because this paradigm's assumptions are so shallow that we must convince ourselves to embrace them again and again and again, same time next year.

Consider the problems these assumptions lead us to.

What does this reasoning suggest about people who have less than I do? Does God think them less faithful, less favored, less loved? Social Darwinists suggest simply that poor people are less intelligent, less motivated, and less able.[4] If Social Darwinists simply blame the poor for their plight, faulty theology goes even further. It blames God! If God will not provide for people who are poor, surely I have no responsibility to do so either. After all, the warped eisegesis has Jesus rationalizing, "You always have the poor with you" (Matt. 26:11).

If this reasoning tempts us to indifference, it also conflates coincidence with providence concerning my own prosperity. If my generosity for God is conditioned upon God's generosity toward me, measured by my prosperity, what am I to conclude should I lose my job, my health, my stock portfolio? If God's blessings toward me decrease, and if my generosity motivator is giving for God, on God's behalf, what shall I do but tighten my generosity belt? That we have come to limit God's blessing to economic prosperity is, of course, merely one more piece of evidence of just how materialistic we are.

Such is the problem with an if/then God. An if/then God inspires if/then disciples. If God blesses me, I will give. If God's blessings diminish, the deal is off.

The story of God we tell conditions the texture of our life together in God, the lives we lead for God. If the problem is sin, the answer is Jesus, and the goal is salvation, the conditional nature of God's love for me may well lead me to a likewise conditional response to God. "God, if you really want me to be generous, prove it. I dare you."

Members of my own faith tradition—the Reformed tradition—will instantly recognize this system as Pelagian and rightly dismiss it out of hand. We most often do not, however, continue our critique long enough to be reminded that biblically, God's project of generosity certainly includes our salvation—thanks be to God!—and yet, God's project of generosity is not limited to my salvation, nor by it. In fact, God's project of generosity as described in Scripture is a breathtaking saga, an edge-of-your-seat drama in which hearts are broken and lives are lost, but not a drama only of sinfulness versus righteousness, salvation versus death. Jesus has come to save us indeed, but not for or from the causes most of us have been taught.

What if sin is *a* problem but not *the* problem?

What if humanity is not *in* God's way but rather God's partner *along* the way?

What if God's goal is not convincing us to love God so that God may in the end swish us away to some other place called heaven? Rather, what if God's goal is inspiring our participation in God's larger effort to return earth to God's dreams for it, to redeem earth for its ultimate unveiling as what it has forever been—our shared destination all along?

As NT Wright has it,

> The central message of the Bible is not simply that we are sinners, but through Jesus God is rescuing us from this sinful world so that we can be with him in heaven. That's part of it, but it's not the whole biblical story. The Bible is not about the rescue of humans from the world but about the rescue of

humans for the world and indeed, God's rescue of the world by means of those rescued humans.[5]

We have just described the kingdom of heaven, the kingdom both necessitated and inspired by the incarnation. This is the promise and the reality that Jesus came to inaugurate. Jesus spoke about God's kingdom more frequently than any other topic, more frequently even than he spoke about money (his second favorite topic). This is the reality that has come near us in Jesus and is even now burgeoning amongst us. The Bible is a story of wild, unleashed generosity, God's generosity, the goal of which is a new heaven and a new earth, eternal communion and bliss, together. Jesus speaks of the kingdom most frequently in the present tense, and, while its complete fulfillment beckons from the horizon, the message is also clear that as Jesus has launched it already, we are to begin living in it now.

Our generosity, therefore, might well be offered for God. We might yet remain stuck in a cycle of transactions, a command-and-respond, blessings-beget-blessings arrangement.

I am convinced, however, that there is a deeper motive for generosity, a motive pure and beautiful, an inspiration at once joyous, doxological, and also transformational. It presumes an understanding and trust in a particular interpretation of the story of God, an interpretation nuanced and different from the predominant reading offered to most American Christians, particularly those of us formed in the Bible belt.

Namely, God's generosity is even now restoring all that we know and have for its final and holy purposes, and we—rattled and frayed though we are—we are invited to participate in the project. Created in God's image, for God's purposes, for God's praise, we have front row seats for the drama of eternity. Our arrangement with God is beyond command-and-response. It is a relationship. God seeks with us a give-and-take, ask-and-answer, exhale-and-inhale partnership.

We are natives in the kingdom of heaven. When we are generous, we echo God, relish God, reflect God. We long to be generous, however, not simply as divine imitation. We long to be generous as participation. Generosity *for* God is good so far as it goes. It is about obedience. Yet we want more.

We want more than to *do generosity*. We want to *become generous*.

We long to be generous alongside God, like God, as God, *with* God. If generosity *for* God is about obedience, generosity *with* God is about identity. When we are generous *with* God, we participate in the sublime progression of God's eternal hopes for the world and for God's people. Our lives contribute to God's divine saga of redemption and reconciliation.

Chapter 3

GENEROSITY *WITH* GOD

"Then the father said to him, 'Son, you are always with me,
and all that is mine is yours.'"

—Luke 15.31

CENTRAL TO JESUS' TEACHINGS, THE PARABLE OF THE PRODIGAL Son is elemental to anyone attempting to follow him. Somewhere I learned—I think from one of my father's sermons—that the parable is misleadingly named. The parable is not about the younger son, at least not at first. It is about the father, about the father whose love is overwhelming, whose forgiveness is overarching, whose generosity is shockingly extravagant. It is about a father who hikes up his robes—a humiliating offense for an otherwise dignified Jewish patriarch—and sprints down the road, gasping and sweating, to embrace his returning son. He cannot help himself. His son has returned from the far country. His son is home. He opens the family's jewelry box and puts a ring on his son's finger and he orders the fatted calf killed. He preps for a party.

The parable caused me no small confusion as a child. My Bible-belt cohorts were telling me that sin is the problem, Jesus is the answer, and my salvation is God's goal. If this is God's story line, and the parable is about the younger son, I was to identify with the sinner-come-home. He wastes his inheritance pursuing wine, women, and song, and still, the father welcomes him home. The message was supposed to be clear. Like that insubordinate boy, I needed to straighten up, fly right, head home.

I had a problem. I didn't identify with the parable's youngest son. I had not asked for my inheritance early. My parents had not liquidated the family wealth on my youthful whim. I had not engaged in particularly profligate living, though a moment or two in college remain a bit iffy. If parables invite us to identify with their characters—at least part of their impact—I felt no particular resonance with the younger son. I was a small-town preacher's kid, a cradle Christian, and a young disciple coloring within the lines, or at least trying to. Mark Twain is purported to have written, "They've got dancing girls, and drinking, and wild parties, and shows here. Virginia City is no place for a Presbyterian. . . . So I am no longer one." Well, I was not profligate. I was Presbyterian. Hence, there was something about this parable that did not speak to me. The extravagantly generous and unexpectedly forgiving father, I understood. Profligate son, not so much.

For those like me, the parable offers one more character to consider. It is the older son.

He never leaves the farm. He serves faithfully without question or complaint, at least not expressed. He works in the fields the very day the scallywag sibling skulks in and the father does not even tell him about the plans for the evening. He hears about the party only from a servant. And he is furious—about the family's tainted reputation, about the father's generosity with the undeserving brother, about the waste of resources he assumes should be his. He refuses to attend.

His father pleads for him to come. The older brother recounts their shared history. He has worked like a slave. He has never disobeyed. He has asked for nothing. Still, "this son of yours" (he is certainly no "brother of mine"!) comes home and Dad throws a prodigal-palooza.

I hardly think that I am alone, identifying as I do with the older brother. Mainline Protestantism, and much of North American Christendom in general, counts itself middle and upper middle class. It is no surprise that we have followed the rules; we wrote them! The entire social and cultural endeavor has our fingerprints all over it, from government to business, from education to economy. We are most of us figurative older brothers and sisters, people who have stuck close to the origins, played by the rules, and remained safely within the family's fence line. Faithfulness has been easily and long defined for us, and for the most part, we have tried to be faithful. It is true that we have left many behind, that we have been blind to our coziness with oppressive systems, that we have ignored much human need. But also, we have tried. We have built our churches, paid our mortgages, confirmed our children, and served our Lord. We have witnessed and underwritten the greatest church expansion spree in our nation's history. We are the good kids, a well-behaved bunch, the silent and selfless masses.

So perhaps you join me, sullen and a bit testy, at the party's entrance? The father hears us out, mind you, entertains our litany about how much we have done and how little we have asked. And we know what will happen when our lips curl in their final assault. We know that our father will wave us in anyway, summon us to celebrate our sibling's return, our oversexed, unkempt, drug-addled, entitled brother's homecoming. But just now, letting our father have a piece of our minds, our spirits clamor for his affirmation, and also, truth told, we long for vindication. What a moment we share with the father, this exchange just outside the banquet hall. My college sculpture professor taught me to sculpt the moment "just before."

If carving the baseball pitcher, capture the second just before he releases the ball. If sculpting the ballerina, depict the millisecond just before she leaps. That is the most telling moment of them all, the moment "just before."

And now, just before we decide if we will join the party, the father speaks. Not only does the father invite us to join the festivities of forgiveness, "You are always with me," he assures us. Then he reminds us of something we are wont to neglect, something so self-evidently true that we haven't noticed it. He continues, "and all that is mine is yours."

If only I had recalled the father's response when my parishioner bragged about God's generosity. "What a generous God," he had said, "who lets me keep ninety percent." I should have said, "God is more generous even than that. All that God has is yours, all ten apples, one hundred percent of it." God holds nothing back. The question is, "How will you use all that God has given you to participate in God's generosity?"

This is the question driving our generosity, at least if we long for a generosity more profound than transacting charity on God's behalf, practicing generosity *for* God. This is the question capable of energizing a generosity practiced alongside God, *with* God. This word—with—delivers a key interpretive lens helpful both in re-envisioning the biblical story and helpful also in imagining a new praxis of generosity.

God's story, voiced in Scripture, centers on God's desire to be with the creation and to be with the creatures God has made. As Sam Wells has written,

> Think back to the very beginning of all things. John's gospel says, "The Word was with God. He was in the beginning with God. . . . Without him not one thing came into being." (John 1:1–3) In other words, before anything else, there was a with. The with between God and the Word, or as Christians came to call it, between the Father and the Son. With is the most fundamental thing about God. And then think about

how Jesus concludes his ministry. His very last words in Matthew's gospel are, "Behold, I am with you always" (28:20). In other words, "There will never be a time when I am not with." And at the very end of the Bible, when the book of Revelation describes the final disclosure of God's everlasting destiny, this is what the voice from heaven says: "See, the home of God is among mortals. He will dwell with them as their God; they will be his peoples, and God himself will be with them" (Rev. 21:3).

We've stumbled upon the most important word in the Bible—the word that describes the heart of God and the nature of God's purpose and destiny for us. And that word is with.[1]

God's deepest desire, God's most generous impulse, is born of the longing to be with us and with the creation. Nothing will keep God at a distance. No gap is so great that God's generosity will not leap it in our direction. At the beginning, within the middle, and at the end, God's story is the ongoing epic of *with*. God yearns for relationship, craves relationship, was born and has died to embrace us within a relationship worthy even of forever, and worthy not only of eternity; worthy of divinity itself. This relationship—this burning, changing, growing, dynamic, progressive relationship—is initiated by God, sustained by God, nourished and tended by God.

I have already labeled this holy desire for relationship an expression of God's innermost generosity. Now we need only understand that our embracing of this relationship inevitably invites us into lifestyles of lavish, extravagant, and dare we say prodigal generosity.

Here we pause to examine why the theology of generosity has so often been neglected by the Christian academy. Branded an offshoot from a larger theology of ecclesiology, or perhaps of discipleship, scholars have too often looked askance at the theology of generosity as little more than fundraising. Many have suspected a theology of stewardship with ulterior motives, a biblical retelling twisted in order simply, cynically, primarily to fund the church. Dirty as a ten-year-old dollar bill, theologians have been slow even to touch it.

Generosity is not best understood, however, as an applied theology of ecclesiology nor of discipleship. Generosity is an applied theology of the doctrine of incarnation, a body of thought concerning our faithful negotiation of the tangible world, the physical world, the earthly world thought of so highly by God that God sought to experience it—both its joys and its limitations. "In Christ God was reconciling the world to himself" (2 Cor. 5:19). God craves to be reconciled with us, and for us to be reconciled with one another, and with the earth. In Christ, through the power of God's Holy Spirit, God will always be with us. God is with us in relationship, where we are, at each and every moment, a wondrous echo of the Trinitarian essence—three persons in one generous and generative relationship.[2]

Should we not be consumed, then, and joyfully so, with the faithful management, use, and sharing of every shred of the tangible within our grasp? Physics tells us that matter is packed with energy, even if motionless to the naked eye. The Bible tells us that matter is the tangible expression of God's creative love. Money is one means of exchanging matter. Money, then, is simply the means of exchange by which humanity determines who gets what, when, where, and how, and perhaps most importantly, who decides. Generosity is the spiritual discipline by which Jesus' followers make and influence these decisions. Disciples make these choices individually and corporately, and the shared nature of generosity is among the church's primary vocations.

There is an old aphorism that "stewardship is everything I do after I say I believe." Authentic generosity is even more elemental than this, however, and certainly antecedent. Stewardship—make that generosity—is everything I give that leads me to know God more deeply.

If practicing generosity *for* God is limited to mere transaction, practicing generosity *with* God is wholly transformational. It is holy transformation. Generosity with God is more
than mere emulation, more than a formulaic duplicating act,
greater even than passionate obedience. To be generous with
God is to become progressively more generous from the heart
to the bone. It is to participate in the very life of God. Generosity is an entrée into God's heart certainly as powerful as forgiveness, or grace, or love, and likely more so, for the simple
reason that generosity is the surest sign that God is transforming us for God's fullest partnership. To practice generosity is to
engage in God's transforming power to make something that
we *do* into something that we *are*. Being generous with God is
a manifestation of our deepest relationship with God.

Think of your own experience of other people. Would you
not say that those who are most generous seem also to know
God most deeply? How could it be otherwise?

Consider the nativity. In a physical outbreaking of incarnate presence, God longed so passionately for relationship
with all that God has created that God births something
wholly new and historically distinct—Jesus the Messiah. With
the glory of a child's birth, omnipotence opted for vulnerability. Omniscience chose self-limitation. God's nature was made
manifest in the enfleshed generosity of coming to be with us,
as a human being.

And consider the cross. No matter your understanding of
atonement—and there are several—the central unifying theme
of the cross of Christ is God's generosity. God in Jesus gave
himself because of us, for us, and to us. In this way and for
this reason, the New Testament continually speaks of Jesus
on the cross as a sacrifice. "For our paschal lamb, Christ, has
been sacrificed" (1 Cor. 5:7). God's decision to become incarnate, and Jesus' willingness to endure the indignity and shame
of death on a cross, and all that Christians understand this

death to mean, are God's central acts of ultimate, sacrificial generosity.

Jesus' birth and crucifixion complete all of God's prior generosities and are foundational to each of God's future generosities. Jesus' sacrificial generosity is, thus, both our redemption and our example. "Therefore be imitators of God, as beloved children, and live in love, as Christ loved us and gave himself up for us, a fragrant offering and sacrifice to God" (Eph. 5:1–2). Jesus is God's generous sacrifice. As his followers, longing to grow more closely into his image, God inspires us to the practice of sacrificial generosity. As we deepen in this practice, we know God more genuinely.

To make a sacrifice is to give something up and away, to set it aside for a more holy purpose. On our behalf, for our benefit, Jesus sacrificed himself upon the cross. This should alert us to our shared experience, then, that when we set aside our possessions and money and perceived self-interest for more holy purposes, we experience God in deepest relationship. When the apostle urges us to "present your bodies as a living sacrifice" (Rom. 12:1), Paul nudges us toward ultimate generosity, toward offering everything—all ten apples—toward God, for God, with God in the ongoing saga of God's redemption and restoration of the world.

Generosity is flowering evidence of our deepest trust in, and friendship with, almighty God. When we are generous with God, we relate most intimately to God, flourish most joyfully toward God, enjoy our deepest relationship with the selfsame father who continues to assure us, "All that I have is yours." The news is this good. The gospel is this expansive, eternal.

Those who are generous with God, those who understand, relish, and participate in God's sacrificial love evidenced from their own generosity, often seem to us most deeply and obviously in relationship with God. They give quietly, humbly, seldom with reward or recognition. Because of their obvious integrity, their generous deeds are never questioned. Neither are their motivations. And while generosity certainly includes sharing one's resources, generosity with God is far more wide-ranging than this. Generosity with God is a posture of the spirit, a temperament toward other people, situations, and toward God. Think of Mother Teresa. Think of the most generous person you know. Generosity includes a kind deed, unexpected, unrequested, unremarkable. Generosity inspires a large tip at a restaurant, or it might listen patiently amidst another's quandary, or it might turn the other cheek. Generosity waits patiently upon the belligerent child and tends lovingly to the aging parent. Generosity absorbs another's criticism without defensiveness, searching their insights for truth. The older I get, the more I value basic kindness, and yet, we must never reduce Christianity to mere kindness, to being gentle, to Pollyannaish platitudes. Still, people possessed of the sacrificial love of God become themselves loving, and forgiving, and gracious, qualities they share bountifully, offer generously.

And this generosity includes money.

All these years later, Oseola McCarty still inspires me. Like many philanthropists discovered suddenly by the secular press, when her story broke in 1995, the news services rushed to print and broadcast the details of her life.

African American, McCarty was born poor and fatherless in rural Mississippi. Living with her mother, grandmother, and an aunt, family responsibilities forced her exit from school in the sixth grade. Like her grandmother, for whom she provided care, she became a washerwoman, an occupation which carried her deep into her eighties when arthritis forced her retirement. In the 1960s she bought a washing machine but got rid of it, preferring to boil her wash water over an open fire and to scrub the cloth by hand. McCarty never married and she had no children. She owned no car, nor, at least until very late in her life, an air conditioner, which she turned on only when guests visited. She subscribed to no newspaper, pushed a grocery cart a mile to the grocery store, and, if it is not yet apparent to you, lived a very modest lifestyle because she made a very modest living. And, she said, she preferred it that way.

And McCarty saved her money. Bank officers contacted McCarty in her eighties, both impressed by and concerned about her mounting wealth. What were her plans for it? Scattering dimes across her kitchen table to represent her accumulated fortune, she outlined the parameters of what would become her irrevocable trust. Three dimes represented the percent designated for her living relatives. One dime denoted the tithe that would go to her church, the Friendship Baptist Church.

Six dimes symbolized the coming bequest that would set the press aflutter, the inspiring news that Oseola McCarty, a poor African American Mississippi washerwoman, would leave $150,000 to the University of Southern Mississippi to underwrite tuition for students who otherwise could not afford the education she had herself been denied. Preference would go to African American students. It was "by far the largest gift ever given to Southern Miss Foundation by an African American."[3] And she would not wait for her death to launch her dream. Immediately her money was set loose. Six hundred neighbors found her generosity so remarkable they added their gifts atop hers. Soon her money more than tripled.

> "Like a lot of philanthropists, Oseola McCarty knew that giving is its own pleasure. When a journalist from *People* magazine asked her why she didn't spend the money she'd saved on herself, she answered with a smile, "I am spending it on myself."[4]

What I find most inspiring and memorable about McCarty's generosity is not merely the modesty and discipline from which it was given. McCarty's motivations were simple and public, offered humbly and frankly. "You have to accept God the best way you know how and then he'll show himself to you. And the more you serve him, the more able you are to serve him." One friend described McCarty's Christian faith as "as simple as the Sermon on the Mount, and as difficult to practice."[5]

Oseola McCarty discovered something of God's generosity and could do nothing less than participate in it, with it, to partner with God known in the world-challenging, sacrificial giving of Jesus. "I just figured the money would do [the scholarship recipients] a lot more good than it would me."[6]

Sacrificial generosity, indeed, and inspiring. Ted Turner— CNN media mogul, yachtsman, businessman—heard about McCarty's generosity. Moved by her example he donated a billion dollars to charity. *The New York Times* quoted Turner on his motivation. "If that little woman can give away everything she has, then I can give a billion."[7]

I know little of Ted Turner's religious affiliations or motivations, and it would be rank silliness to argue that only religious people are generous. What strikes me is his recognition of holiness when he sees it. When Jesus' disciples are generous *with* God, we are transformed. And we are more; we are transformational. By measurable standards the philanthropy of billionaires might make a bigger difference than that of poor people, but when it comes to inspiration, give me Oseola McCarty, not Ted Turner. The gospel isn't about measuring things that rot or rust. Jesus seems to agree, given his attention to the widow's mite in the temple.

It is easy to scour history and newspapers for examples like Mother Teresa and Oseola McCarty, yet as a pastor I need look no further than my congregation's giving records for illustrations of the powerful truth that generosity is often the most obvious outgrowth of an intimate relationship with

God. Christianity is always practiced within congregations—simple, run-of-the-mill congregations. Kevin Van Hoozer writes that the local congregation is "the location or place where the rule of God breaks into and thus begins to change the world."[8] In my experience, those with whom I worship who have also engaged a lifestyle of intentional generosity, those who have shared sacrificially for the church's mission and for more, those most possessed of the idea that surely "the Lord is my shepherd, I shall not want," these saints are also liberal in spirit, generous at their very core.

What follows then is no accident. They are also likeliest to "encourage the faint-hearted," to "help the weak," and to "be patient with all of them." They are most resistant to repaying "evil for evil." They seem always to "seek to do good to one another and to all." They "rejoice always" and against the odds they "pray without ceasing." They "give thanks in all circumstances" (1 Thess. 5:14–18). They are, shall we say, Christians.

Which is not to say that stingy disciples are not Christians. The church includes many selfish people too, people fearful and miserly, disciples anxious and close-handed. If not for heaven's sake then at least for mine, the church also welcomes even people like me, and you, even and especially ungenerous people who are also nonetheless welcome to the Table. We just do not understand it, not yet anyway, not fully. Such understanding takes time, and often, it takes a divine nudge, sometimes a painful nudge.

This is the moment to admit that generosity, precisely because it is transformational, is not always easy. In fact, a generous spirit is frequently hard-won, forged in the fires of despair and crisis. Transformation, after all, often emerges from contention, arises even from death. Theologically speaking, the old earth must give way to the new, the old heart make room for the fresh heart.

Raley Taliaferro shared with me the story of her own journey to generosity and the parts of her very self that had to die along the way. She worshiped in the last congregation I served.[9]

On the first day of her freshman year, Raley's mother drove her to high school. She wore new clothes, the family's annual ritual, purchased for the coming academic year. Her outfit included new shoes. In the backseat sat Raley's younger brother Addison Pierce, a seventh grader, likewise awarded a new wardrobe, only he had not put on his new shoes. He wore his old pair, his new shoes untouched in their box, perched upon his lap. Glancing back their mother noticed and commented. "Mom," Addison replied, "my friend has no money for new shoes. May I give him mine?" It was a telling moment, a simple and revealing instant, exposing deepest character and honest convictions. "Of course," their mother said, and while little else was said about the exchange, something true and exquisite had been revealed, both about Addison's nature and about their mother's.

Years passed. In high school Addison's behavior changed. A shy kid who loved animals, Addison had been admitted to the Gifted and Talented Program based upon his essay, written at age 8, entitled, "My Life as a Cereal Box." Now, his grades slipped. He began having trouble with adults, including the police. He hung with a tough crowd. He became uncharacteristically belligerent and withdrawn. At 18 Addison was diagnosed: bipolar schizoaffective disorder. He experienced audible hallucinations, a frightening reality not only for Addison but for his entire family. Nonetheless they rallied around Addison as he graduated from high school and took a job.

Addison stabilized, though life was a constant balancing act between medications, a seek-and-find effort to learn which medications, in what combination and sequence, would allow Addison his most comfortable and controlled life. His behavior mellowed with medication and with age. He met a woman and fell in love, and together they welcomed a daughter.

Raley was with her father the day they found Addison's body. He had died from an unintentional overdose of prescription medication. Raley, now an only child at 25, helped plan his funeral, conducted in a local funeral home so as not to leave grief's mark upon the sanctuary where the family regularly worshiped.

And Raley spiraled into a personal, emotional, and existential crisis. She became depressed, lounging for long periods, staying inside, at home, sleeping the afternoons away on the couch. She sought treatment, and therapy, which seemed to help, but still, something was missing. She was not healing.

Reflecting in my study at the church, she said, "I felt grief was such a selfish process, and I was so angry with God. I knew that to get better, I was going to have to work my peace with God."

Suddenly an idea came to her. It was not her idea, Raley says, but the idea of another, from somewhere outside of her. "When the idea occurred to me," Raley said, "I knew it was God." She had not thought for years about Addison's seventh grade shoes, and suddenly that moment leapt to consciousness with redemptive creativity. She would create a project to honor Addison and to help others. It would mirror Addison in that long ago moment, and she would name the effort Give SOLES—Serving Our Lord Every Step. It was only an idea, a subject without an object, a vision seeking a target, but soon, the concept took aim at a local boy's home. Raley approached the executive director, whom she did not know, with the simple request to buy shoes for the residents.

Give SOLES took form and flight. Five years later, with tax-free status in hand, Raley Taliaferro and Give SOLES have raised over $100,000 to purchase shoes for family-less boys. They have restored the athletic fields at the boy's home, installed soccer goals and basketball hoops, and more. The athletic complex at the home has been named the Addison Pierce Toliver Complex. "While Addison's death was disappointing," Raley reflects, "Addison was not."

When Addison died, Raley had been obsessed with establishing herself in the professional world. "I was so focused on ridiculous things, unimportant things, business things," she says. "Addison's death woke me up to what most matters."

When Raley shared with me the details of Addison's story, and hers, I was struck by her thoughtfulness, her pensive awareness born clearly of deep thought and remarkable conviction. This is a story she has told before—not too often, clearly, for to do so might somehow cheapen it, make it less holy. Having revealed the storyline, her eyes shifted to the right, away from my eyes, and Raley Taliaferro uttered what seemed to me a new thought, one that can necessarily come only in retrospect, by looking back. Seeing God in the present is a learned skill cultivated by noticing God in the past. Adam sees God only as God walks away in the garden. Moses sees God only as God departs, peaking from the cleft rock (Exod. 33:23). Raley realized something in my study as if for the first time, looking back. "When I didn't feel God," she said, "the idea of being generous brought God back to me. That is how God healed me."

Generosity is evidence of an authentic relationship with God. It also ushers us into fuller relationship with God's people. Our connections blossom alongside those whose lives are touched by God's generosity, particularly when that generosity is made visible through our own. In other words, God joins us to those with whom we are generous. Generosity is the nexus, the center point, of our most life-giving relationships— our vertical relationships with the divine and our horizontal relationships with human beings. This is part of the transformational power of generosity. It's quite simply described:

generosity changes people. It changes those who give and it changes those who receive.

When we are generous with God, God transforms those with whom we are generous.

Stephanie Bullock, a black high school senior when Oseola McCarty made her $150,000 gift to Southern Miss, hoped to go to college. She was president of the senior class and a good student, but her grades were not enough to win an academic scholarship. Her parents earned just enough to disqualify her for government grants and too little to pay for her college. And, Bullock has a twin brother who aspired to college also. College was a dream worthy of her abilities and her dreams, but it appeared to be just out of reach. Then Bullock received the news that she was the first chosen to receive McCarty's scholarship. It was, she said, a "miracle" and an "honor."[10]

Four years later Bullock completed the undergraduate degree funded by McCarty. In fact, she was in graduate school when McCarty, whom she called Miss Ola, died in 1999. Bullock eulogized McCarty in *Time* magazine. The last sentence of her article reads, "I hope to live a life comparable to hers."[11]

This is the power of generosity with God. McCarty embraced God's generosity and partnered with it in the world. Ms. Bullock embraced McCarty's generosity and committed herself to a life of the same.

We have framed the biblical narrative as the saga of God's generosity. We have observed that our generosity takes two forms: an initial response, generosity *for* God, which limits us to transaction, and generosity *with* God, which engages us in transformation and prepares us within for fuller relationship with God. We have celebrated that *for* can lead to *with*, that treasure leads our hearts and not the other way around. And, we have observed that when we engage in relationship with partners in our generosity, *with* awakens us to more than we had dreamt. The ultimate *with* is God. God is with us in our generosity. And God joins us in relationship with those our generosity helps to prosper.

Here is generosity's fullest significance. Every act of sharing, every word spoken within generous relationships, every exchange initiated within liberality, every thought and every dollar offered sacrificially opens our eyes to the broader vista of God's ongoing restoration of the world, God's eternal and ongoing ministries of reconciliation and redemption. We are more than mere tools for God's generosity. *We are God's partners.* We are collaborators in a conscious vision of what the world is meant for, where the world is heading—by and in God's grace, through and because of the work of Jesus Christ.

We are meant for life abundant in the kingdom. From the moment we are born, we are meant to be generous with God.

Part II

The Power of Generosity . . .

IF GOD'S GENEROSITY IS THE *WHAT* OF OUR CONVERSATION, THE *so what* is the cultural context within which we practice generosity with God. What is that setting?

I no longer tell seatmates on airplanes that I am a minister. Neither my faith nor my profession embarrass me. Nonetheless, when people discover my vocation, their reactions are inevitably twofold, neither of which is particularly fruitful.

Sometimes news of my profession evokes an impromptu counseling session, invites a detailed outpouring of my fellow traveler's life and its numerous troubles, all of which I would be willing to discuss in my study, but not on an airplane. I am stunned by the salacious details travelers will proffer within earshot of shocked strangers. (A seatmate once confided to me her guilt about a recent ménage à trois, wholly unconcerned with who might overhear. WWJD, indeed!)

Other times the revelation of my reverend-ness unleashes a pent-up antagonism toward all of Christianity and the church. Years ago my seatmate let loose with a sophomoric diatribe about the Christian faith and those who try to practice it. "Christianity is a farce," he began. "The resurrection is a delusional retrojection. It never happened." He was just getting started. "The church is full of hypocrites. Christians are very critical. Christians are so judgmental. The church is chockfull of people who say one thing and do another." And on he went.

Finally, I interrupted him. "Look," I said, "you have to stop. You're talking about my people. I live and breathe and spend most of my time in the church, and with church folks. They are my friends. They are my family. They are my parishioners and my employers. I know a lot of them and a lot about them. Oh, the stories I could share about the church."

Then I said, "And let me tell you, it is much worse than you think."

That shut him down.

I continued, "And still, the church is the best game in town."

It is true. The church's hypocrisy and shortcomings are so obvious precisely because the church aspires to divinity. Every Sunday we join our voices to recommit as God's agents to make "earth as it is in heaven." With such lofty goals, then, falling short is painfully public and embarrassingly visible. For those who do not know the church well, or only from a distance, and for those who have been scorned or hurt by the church, the delta between the institution's aspiration and its actuality is more than dispiriting. It is more than off-putting. It is a moral offense.

The American church is awakening to the public's perceptions of it, and this is one of the reasons that the church is changing. It must. We must. The culture is changing too. Change is all there is, of course, so this is news to no one.

What is newsworthy is the culture's growing indifference toward the Christian church, disrespect even. Within the lifespan of many of my parishioners, the church has fallen from an upright perch of near universal respect and authority to a position of struggle and insecurity. And while our congregations are shrinking (by the way, denominations do not lose members, congregations do) proportionate to the culture's suspicion of them, here is the truth: American culture has never more needed the church to be authentically faithful to the core of the gospel.

God's generosity is at the core of the gospel. God's generosity is the heartbeat of the gospel. American culture in the twenty-first century needs desperately to know a God capable of lifting it from the greedy, self-aggrandizing, and materialistic idols it has concocted for itself. If sin is most basically selfishness, generosity is sin's antidote. Generosity is God's example and God's gift. Generosity is countercultural, world-shaking, eye-dropping, and dare I say it? Redemptive.

In this section I consider the power of practicing generosity with God. I will reflect upon generosity's demonstrable power: to inspire gratitude, to clarify want versus need, to redirect our economic gaze, as an antidote to the chief idols of the age, as an ancient and primary spiritual discipline, and as the believer's call.

Chapter 4

. . . TO INSPIRE GRATITUDE

I WAS SPEAKING ABOUT GENEROSITY AT A KENTUCKY GATHERING and broached, just before the scheduled coffee break, perhaps the touchiest stewardship subject of them all. The tallest hurdle between fear and generosity for most people, I observed, is the pervasive anxiety that we will not have enough. In the wealthiest nation the world has ever known, still we find reason to doubt the psalmist when he declares, "The Lord is my shepherd; I shall not want." I asked, "Do we actually believe that?" Then the crowd disbursed for coffee and cinnamon rolls.

I used the intermission to check my phone messages. These were the days before smartphones and my cranky black screen booted so very slowly. I had gotten the phone only the day before, so I was just learning to use it. Its startup screen sported the carrier's corporate logo, in this case AT&T, and I was amazed to see two unexpected words flash just beneath the logo. They appeared for three or four seconds, then vanished. They came and went so quickly that I actually rebooted the phone just to see if my mind and eyes had colluded to confuse me. The second startup showed the same unexpected message: God provides.

I first wondered why AT&T would offer such an explicitly religious message on its cellphones. It seemed strangely out of character. The only other possibility was that God's winsome Holy Spirit is computer literate and had digitized the exact message I then most needed to see and say.

Now, I am a child of enlightenment rationalism, so neither option—AT&T *or* YHWH—seemed particularly plausible. Still, I had seen it with my own eyes. Doubting Thomas that I am, I had little choice but to share the story with the regathered assembly. "I don't know how this happened," I concluded, "but the message is right on time and good as gold." The crowd howled with laughter.

Several weeks passed. I gave little additional thought to the mobile phone miracle. Then Madelene, my then middle school daughter, said to me, "Did you get my message on your phone?" Mystery solved. Madelene had programmed my startup screen.

I replied, "Madelene, it was wonderful." I told her about the message's sublime timing. Then I asked, "But of all the messages you could have chosen, why "God provides"?

"It is the thing I have the hardest time believing."

"Step, my child," I heard myself thinking, "into this anxiety I have prepared for you." Here I was traipsing around the country pontificating on God's generosity, and obviously I was living in such a way that my own children had their doubts. It was a clarifying and human moment. Obviously, I must participate in the shared anxiety, that we won't have enough.

I am convinced that trust in God's provision is often proportionate to our awareness of it. The opposite of faith is not, after all, doubt. It is fear. We fear scarcity, and many live in abundance they do not name as abundance. Gratitude can open our eyes. Gratitude peels the scales of fear away and reveals to us the nature and breadth of God's blessings. Think Scrooge on Christmas morning, and George Bailey in Frank Capra's *It's a Wonderful Life*, and Zacchaeus after he climbs down from the tree (Luke 19:8).

If gratitude can awaken us to our abundance, generosity can awaken us to our gratitude.

You have no doubt heard the words gratitude and generosity linked. Connecting them is far more than good alliteration. We normally combine the words in this order: gratitude first, then generosity. Count your blessings, the thinking goes, and then you'll be moved to share. Being thankful is the initial step toward being generous, we say. How many stewardship sermons have closed with the assertive charge to count our blessings, confident that doing so will up our pledge?

I will hand it to you that this sequence is an authentic spiritual inspiration. Gratitude can indeed lead to generosity. It is especially true when material blessings are mounting, when incomes are growing, when bank accounts are swelling. Material blessings have mounted throughout American history. That is the core impulse of the American dream, after all, to give our children more than we had. More. Always more. With prosperity on the rise, counting blessings is indeed a compelling generosity motivator.

But my generation, economists say, will be the first American generation to fare economically less well than our parents. Teaching us, then, that generosity flows from gratitude, and then linking gratitude with ever-growing personal wealth, is a recipe for spiritual heartburn and disconnection.

If gratitude and generosity are linked, is it possible that generosity might come first? Might it be that first we are generous, and that authentic gratitude might follow? Many a liturgist has called for the Sunday offering by intoning the apostle

Paul: "Each of you must give as you have made up your mind, not reluctantly or under compulsion, for God loves a cheerful giver" (2 Cor. 9:7). Does God also love a grumpy giver, love an ungrateful and grouchy giver?

It is counterintuitive, I suppose, that generosity might produce gratitude. Yet would you not agree that the most powerful spiritual disciplines are always self-confirming? We cannot know why we ought to pray unless and until we pray. We cannot appreciate the benefits of worship unless and until we worship. Sometimes we do what we are called to do because it is only in the doing of it that we discover why we are to have done it. So it is with generosity.

I officiated the funeral of a 53-year-old woman, Virginia Tate. Her death was an attack out of season, ovarian cancer at its most evil and indiscriminate. She was a delightful person, loved by all, beautiful and ebullient. She glowed with joy. She was gentle in nature though assertive when necessary. She was no one's pushover. And she was known broadly for her generous spirit. Her family was generous with the church they joined and the schools their children attended. This woman also created remarkable needlepoint items—always with joy, often for friends—for graduations, at births, at weddings. Her 500-plus handmade gifts are cherished and displayed across the country.

The guiding question behind every funeral meditation I preached was, "What have we learned about the Divine, through this person, that otherwise we might not have known?" Sitting with her widowed husband and two sons, planning her funeral, a familiar quote framed this saint's life. When her boys were young, she would serve them the meal she had prepared and, if they complained about the green beans or the entrée, she would gently say, "You get what you get, and you say thank you." We laughed at the retelling.

Then I spoke with her students. She had been a longtime kindergarten teacher and her students, many of them by then in college, returned to tell me stories about her. "We would complain about something," they shared, "and she would always say, 'You get what you get, and you say thank you.'"

I suddenly understood the covenant she made with her husband Wally the day she received the cancer diagnosis. They had left the doctor's office and gone home for the evening, and over the course of it they found their way to a shared prayer. They asked God to use her cancer, and her struggle against it, to somehow bless others as God would choose.

You get what you get—green beans or cancer—and you say thank you, not for the cancer, but for its lessons, for its unexpected opportunities, for God's very goodness in its midst, and all of it amidst a lifetime of gratitude. It was as if her entire life of faith had led to that single crystalline instant, a moment met so often with fear and anger, but in her life a moment to prepare, somehow, to give to others, and to say thank you.

You *get* what you *give, then* you say thank you. Generosity leads to gratitude. Or at least it can.

God unleashed this reality upon me early in my ministry and parenting. Our first child had arrived. The church's health care company was months behind processing claims. Not hearing from the insurer, the local hospital began sending bills for the remaining hospital expenses directly to me. The first bill arrived 60 days past due. The second, 90 days past due.

I knew nothing to do but to pay the bill and hope for eventual reimbursement. The problem was that we didn't have the money to pay the bill, unless, that is, we sent to the hospital the money we had saved toward our church pledge. Looking back, the choice seems less urgent or stark than it did at the time. We knew then only that the decision seemed Faustian, that compromising our covenantal commitment with God's community seemed out-of-bounds.

So, we found another solution. We decided to sell our second car. It was a 1981 Chevrolet Citation, an awful car even when it was new, and ours was quite old. Old and tired. I detailed it as well as it could be detailed. Inside and out, I scrubbed, waxed, and polished, and then I drove it to a used car lot to see how much it was worth. I sat in the passenger's seat as the proprietor took it for a drive. He said little, but when we pulled back into his parking lot, he offered me his price. His offer matched the hospital bill, to the penny.

It is easy to confuse coincidence with providence, and even now I'm not sure which of these this was. And, if you expect me to share next that another car miraculously appeared as if to reward us for the risk of paying the church pledge, that is not how the story ends. We paid our pledge. We did without a second car. Pollyanna made no appearance.

But God did. In those next months, our integrity intact and our values in motion, I found myself unusually grateful for all that we possessed, tangible and intangible. Counting my blessings became as easy and regular as breathing. I was a bit grumpy when the offering plate passed, knowing the inconvenience and risk it necessitated, but I had never felt more loved by my Maker, more in sync with God's heartbeat, or more grateful. Risky generosity had led to a deeper level of gratitude. Generosity can make us grateful.

Chapter 5

. . . TO CLARIFY
WANT VERSUS NEED

SELLING MY 1981 CHEVY CITATION DID MORE THAN CONNECT ME to a buried gratitude. It also revealed to me another truth. If generosity can lead to gratitude, generosity can also clarify what we need from what we merely want. While it was inconvenient for a married couple with a newborn child to live without a second car, I learned also that it can be done, and relatively easily. (The majority of people in the world do it, after all.)

What is true, then, of an '81 Chevy is true of many things. We often crave more than we actually need. Much, much more.

Have you noticed the human tendency to want more and ever more? Remember the old Lay's potato chip commercial: "You can't eat just one." More is good. Big is better. If we keep eating, someday, we might get full. Well, Elon Musk is chasing the next deal and Warren Buffet refuses to retire. We can never satiate the insatiable.

Biblically, this is what Jesus is stabbing at when he observes that it is as hard for a rich person to enter God's kingdom as for a camel to saunter through the eye of a needle. Jesus is not being prescriptive. He is not prescribing that all rich people are hell bound. Jesus is being descriptive. He is describing what he sees. Jesus observes that when good people become accustomed to the things wealth buys, we can forget what is most important. Having a heart *of* gold and having a heart *for* gold are mostly incompatible. Oh, a few have managed both, but generally, people nurture a heart *for* gold while telling themselves that they will become generous when they're well off. It rarely works out that way. Wealth often perpetuates an appetite for more of it, for more things, and things rust and rot.

Which explains a great deal about our culture. Recall the parable of the Rich Fool (Luke 12:13–21). His barns are bursting yet there is more grain to store, so he proposes bigger barns and he prepares to "eat, drink, and be merry." The parable ends in God's voice; "You fool! This very night your life is being demanded of you. And the things you have prepared, whose will they be?" (v. 20).

Well, it is nighttime in America. We have built ever larger barns only to discover that filling them has cost some good portion of our souls. The average size of the American home between 1950 and 2019, the last year for which data is currently available, rose from 983 square feet to 2,301 square feet, a 134 percent increase, and this in a time when the American family was shrinking.[1] By 2019, almost half of all single-family American homes built had four bedrooms. Or more.[2] The median price of a new American home between 1980 and 2022 rose 573 percent.[3] We financed these homes with ever riskier mortgages until the entire house of cards collapsed with the 2008 crash, and analysts in 2022 are warning of yet another developing housing bubble preparing to pop.

Bigger homes. Bigger mortgages. Bigger credit card balances. All of these have informed the remainder of our pecuniary expectations. Over time, we have accumulated with little notice bigger wardrobes, grander vacations, and larger waistlines. Gallup relates that the self-reported weights of American adults is up 20 pounds in as many years.[4] We have become fat and happy, except that every survey I read on the subject reports that we are less happy. In fact, one longitudinal study, the General Social Survey, has "collected data on American attitudes and behaviors at least every other year since 1972."[5] Its most recent survey (June 2020) revealed the lowest percentage of Americans reporting being "very happy" (fourteen percent) than at any time over the last 50 years.[6]

When I began thinking and speaking about generosity and stewardship in the 1990s, the nation's economy was soaring. Recent college graduates were cashing paychecks their parents had waited decades to earn. The stock market hovered at record levels. Dot-coms were flying high. Unemployment was low, inflation was even lower, and the gross domestic product was expanding at a more than decent rate. By 1998, even the federal government was running a surplus budget.

In the 1990s the generosity conversation concentrated on sharing from our abundance. Most families had more than enough. Our basic needs being met, being generous with God presumed the capacity to distinguish between what we authentically need and what we merely want.

In 2008, most everything changed. The economic mood soured. If 9/11 had not been enough to shake our economic confidence, the burst of the housing bubble and the subsequent meltdown of the financial system brought our nation closer to economic disaster than most people want to realize. Both the public and the private sectors took draconian measures to shore up our complex financial networks. Unemployment skyrocketed. Bankers could not keep up with mortgage defaults. Housing values nose-dived, often plunging a home's value beneath what its owner owed on it. Suddenly everyone knew the meaning of being "upside down." Education debt outpaced even consumer debt. Consumer confidence dropped. Anxiety became a leading economic indicator, and around American's kitchen tables, and in America's pews, the generosity conversation shifted from sharing from our abundance to sharing from our substance.

In the 1990s, we spoke of generosity amidst prosperity. Following 2007, we spoke of generosity amidst austerity.

As I write this book, COVID-19 has again changed our economic outlook. Inflation is on the rise even though unemployment is at record lows. Young workers are often relegated to the gig economy while defined benefits pension plans are things of the past. There is now no such thing as 40 years with the same company, then a gold watch. Whole sectors are giving rise to entirely new ways to generate wealth, from professional YouTubers to the expansion of cryptocurrencies. Wealth disparity is greater than at any time since the Gilded Age.

And still, these shifts—from prosperity to austerity, from abundance to substance—do not necessitate much of a generosity rethink at all. The idea that generosity is different in lean times from flush simply masks an underlying economic and theological reality.

Namely, God calls Jesus' followers to generous lifestyles no matter our economic status, no matter the state of the economy. This was true prior to the Great Recession and it is true after it. I will hand it to you that the texture of a millionaire's generosity will be different from the generosities practiced by a fast-food worker. It is true, also, that a family's generosity will take different forms and proportions after a layoff. Still, whether we are wealthy, poor, or somewhere in between, disciplined generosity plays a clarifying spiritual role in every disciple's life. Generosity helps to distinguish between what we need and what we merely want.

Ask ten Christians their favorite Bible verse and at least one of them will likely offer Paul's observation that "I can do all things through him who strengthens me" (Phil. 4:13). As inspirational as this is, it is too often plucked out of its fullest context. "Not that I am referring to being in need," the apostle begins, "for I have learned to be content with whatever I have. I know what it is to have little, and I know what it is to have plenty. In any and all circumstances I have learned the secret of being well-fed and of going hungry, of having plenty and of being in need" (Phil. 4:11–12). It is now—and only now—that Paul offers his tagline for our refrigerator doors: "I can do all things through him who strengthens me." Paul can confidently "do all things" in Christ because his generosity in service has taught him the distinction between need and want. Paul has learned to be content.

A work team from First Presbyterian Church in Fort Worth volunteered at a Haitian orphanage. In their dormitory they found this sign, clearly aimed at First World visitors: "If you cannot find something you need, ask us. We will show you how you can do without it."

We live in a culture which proffers wants as needs. From Madison Avenue to Main Street, producers and merchants must convince us to purchase their products, their services, or both. This cycle of production and consumption, of accumulation and then more, has shaped Americans, Christians included.

Paradoxically, study after study reveals that Americans with lower incomes—and therefore presumably higher need—give the highest percentage of their incomes to church and charity. Maybe this is because when we have less, risking it seems less consequential. Kris Kristofferson told us that "freedom's just another word for nothin' left to lose."[7] Jesus tells us that if we lose our life for his sake, we will find our life (Matt. 10:39). Regardless of why, it is simply demonstrable that poorer Americans are more generous than richer Americans.

Maybe you have heard about the wealthy woman who celebrated that when she first started out, she tithed a full ten percent to her church. "Now," she admitted to her pastor, "I make hundreds of thousands of dollars every year. A tithe on that amount is huge. I can no longer afford to tithe." Her pastor immediately led her into prayer, asking God to reduce her income so that she could afford to tithe again.

There is a similar joke about the layman who was moved to speak in worship on Stewardship Sunday. "You all know," he began, "that I am the wealthiest man in town. I have a grand home and fine cars. My family takes European vacations and we live a wonderful lifestyle. You may not know, however, why this wealth has come my way." The man continued in a smug and self-assured way. "The answer is—God. God has blessed me. God has blessed me because, long ago, I gave all that I had to God. You see, just after starting my first job, on the day I received my first pay, I went to church. The sermon was excellent, the music sublime, and, when the offering plate passed my way, I was so moved that I put my pay in the plate, all of it. Because I gave all that I had, God has blessed me all these years. But first, I had to risk it all." He sat down, superior and secure and untouchable.

The woman next to him leaned over and quietly whispered, "Dare you to do it again."

How hard it is to give it all when we have so much to give. And yet, we ponder a fascinating question: Why do poorer Americans share more of what they have?

The first answer, commonly theorized, is that poorer Americans personally witness greater need. Living in disadvantaged neighborhoods, frequently exposed to human privation, their empathy is regularly tapped. They are moved to generosity because they are surrounded by people who will benefit from it.

The second theory is that, having shared to meet the authentic needs around them, they have learned to make do with what they have. Confronted with needs greater than their own, they have reordered their perceptions and reprioritized what most matters to them. Thankful for their blessings, their wants become clear from their needs.

I have heard many times from survivors of the Great Depression something akin to, "What we need now is another Depression." They do not believe this, not literally, and yet their imaginations leap back to a time when they experienced authentic community, shared responsibility amidst shared need, and genuine generosity. While they remember the challenges and anxieties, the deprivations and hardships of the Great Depression, they also remember a clinging to basic human goodness that they find missing today.

It seems a spiritual law: the less we have, the more we give. In 1921, "church members of eleven primary Protestant denominations (or their historical antecedents) in the United States and Canada" gave 2.9 percent of their incomes to charity.[8] By 2000, with a prosperous economy, members in those same churches gave 2.6 percent, a lower percentage. More striking, however, is the fact that in one year of the eighty-year stretch between 1921 and 2000, income plummeted to its lowest point. That year was 1933. In 1933, American incomes hit rock bottom. Paradoxically, per member giving in those same churches was not 2.6 percent as it was in 2000, or 2.9 percent as it was in 1921. In 1933, per member giving was 3.3 percent.[9] This is the reality that Depression survivors recall—sacrificial generosity amidst devastating and shared scarcity.

If it is true that the less we have, the more we give, the reverse is also true, at least statistically; the more we have, the less we give. The Science of Generosity Survey, taken in 2010, reveals that Americans who make more than $90,000 per year gave on average 1.1 percent of their income to charities. The same survey shows that Americans who make the least, less than $12,499 per year, gave away exactly twice the percentage of their incomes (2.2 percent).[10]

The patterns seem true over time. The less we have, the more we give. Think of the widow's mite (Mark 12:41–44 and Luke 21:1–4).

Conversely, the more we have, the less we give. Think of the rich young ruler (Matt. 19:16–30, Mark 10:17–31, Luke 18:18–30).

To observe these tendencies is not to castigate wealth or wealthy people, though stewarding wealth clearly brings both responsibility and temptation. Likewise, it is not to romanticize poverty nor to heap patronizing praise on people who are poor. There is nothing intrinsically noble about poverty. People of modest means sharing more sacrificially than their wealthy counterparts illustrates generosity's power to refine the giver's heart and desires. Somehow, when we share like God shares, we think more precisely about what we actually need. Such is the spiritual alchemy of emulating God.

And, when people—rich or poor—become more aware of the human need around them, they are likelier to give increasing portions of their incomes. In fact, research shows a compelling link between increased generosity among the wealthy when people of means are made aware of human needs.[11] Bluntly, it is probable that wealthy people share less simply because we live insulated lives. Upper and upper-middle class people—which describes a good portion of American Mainline Protestants—cling to our money because we are removed from the great need all around us.

Which leads us to yet one more element in the case for generosity's power.

Chapter 6

. . . TO REDIRECT
OUR ECONOMIC GAZE

GENEROSITY REDIRECTS OUR ECONOMIC GAZE, INSPIRING US TO contrast down rather than to compare up.

What is comparing up? Comparing up is breaking the last of the Ten Commandments, "You shall not covet" (Exod. 20:17a).

Ever notice how much time employees spend fulfilling the last item on their job descriptions, the bullet that reads "other duties as assigned"? The final sentence in the tenth commandment is like the final bullet on many job descriptions, which cues us to how hard it will be, and how much time it will take, to obey the commandment. "You shall not covet your neighbor's house; you shall not covet your neighbor's wife, or male or female slave, or ox, or donkey, *or anything that belongs to your neighbor*" (Exod. 20:17, emphasis mine). Anything else. Other duties as assigned. You shall not long for your neighbor's spouse or your neighbor's ox or donkey or Lexus or wardrobe or Rolex or business card or 1040 Tax Form. Think about what it would look like if Americans took this commandment seriously.

After all, consumerism is built upon covetousness. Consumerism depends upon, feeds upon, our desire to gaze up the economic ladder. At root, every billboard, every newspaper and magazine ad, every television commercial and pop-up advert is designed either to make us feel inadequate or to stoke the competitive spirit with our neighbor. Keeping up with the Joneses, we call it.

Years ago I bought the newest car I had then ever owned. It was a used car but it was only one year old. I was so proud of it. Several months later the family across the street, named Jones, bought the exact model car, in the same color, only theirs was brand new, and two model-years newer. "That's new," I thought. "The Joneses are keeping up with me."

This desire to compare and compete, this longing for what others have, this impulse to define our need not by the actual realities of our lives but upon a compulsive instinct to have the same or better possessions as other people, is spiritual cancer. It destroys souls. I know adult men who resent their brothers for making more money than they do. I know a woman who lost her marriage to her husband's incredulity that she wanted to spend $250,000 on a kitchen redo to match the couple across the street.

In deep and frightening ways, our entire consumerist economy depends upon the intentional conjuring of old-fashioned covetousness. We want what others have, and because the supply of other people, and their possessions, is near infinite, we seem always to be wanting. We want more and more. It leads to the ordering of our spirits and our lifestyles around wanting and seeking more.

This is comparing up. It is nothing new. Biblically, it is simple, old-fashioned covetousness. It stands in stunning contrast to the gospel of Jesus Christ.

Consider Jesus, relying upon the generosity of strangers.

Picture him with the widow who gives a mite, heralding her trust that despite all other appearances, God will provide for her even amidst her poverty. Note too the implicit condemnation of the rich who allow a widow to exist in such poverty.

Remember his words about the birds of the air, and the flowers of the field, about trusting that God will provide what we need. Not more than we need. Not stockpiles in embarrassing proportion to what we need. Rather, what we need.

Remember the rich fool, his barns bursting and his ears ringing with God's words, "You fool! This very night your life is being demanded of you. And the things you have prepared, whose will they be?" (Luke 12:20).

Jesus suggests a complete reversal of fortunes. Jesus wants his followers to stop comparing up the economic ladder, to stop longing and lusting and coveting for what others have, and to start contrasting downwards, to notice and associate with those yet below on that economic ladder.

I know a Presbyterian mission coworker who spent years in South America and Mexico. At one of his posts, he and his wife hired a local woman. They did not usually hire such help, but she was very poor and needed the money. So, they acted upon their desire to share with her while respecting her need for self-sufficiency. They hired her to clean their house.

Her first payday came. My friend paid her in cash. She left his home, the screen door slamming as she crossed the wooden porch, and walked across the yard, and into the dirt street, where she happened across another woman. She stopped. They spoke. My friend watched his house cleaner reach into her pocket and give the passerby all the money he had just paid her.

He ran to the street, and, when they were alone, asked her, "Why did you do that? That was your money."

With an earnest honesty, she turned to him and replied in Spanish, "But sir, she needs that money. She is poor."

Comparing up is covetousness. It produces jealous emptiness. It draws the eye away from one's blessings and plants a cancerous discontent.

Contrasting down cures covetousness. It flips the world topsy-turvy. Turning our gaze from those with more to those with less, we become more aware of, and more thankful for, God's blessings in our own lives. We become thankful for what we have and less concerned with what we do not.

Better yet, contrasting down stokes our empathy and inspires our generosity. By evoking our empathy for those who have less, contrasting down inspires our generosity with them. When our generosity intersects other people's needs, we have partnered with God in healing the world. Then, "thy kingdom come, thy will be done, on earth as it is in heaven" leaves our lips less a prayer than a promise. We have become God's generous partners.

Chapter 7

... TO DETHRONE THE CHIEF IDOLS OF THE AGE

THE CHIEF IDOLS OF OUR AGE ARE NOT SUBSTANTIVELY DIFFERENT from those of Jesus's age, though we have certainly zealously lifted them into our cultural pantheon. They are materialism, consumerism, and acquisition. I am convinced that vibrant and thoughtful congregational generosity programs can be subversive attempts to undermine our culture's luring us headlong into materialistic, consumeristic, and acquisitive lifestyles.

We all know what consumerism is, of course. Consumerism is buying things we do not need with money we do not have to impress people we do not like.[1]

In a sermon I once described my family's attempt at helping a drug addicted homeless man. We fed him. We washed his clothes. We paid him to do household chores. The very first time we left him alone in our home, he stole our lawnmower. "Poverty," I observed in that sermon, "does terrible things to people." After the worship service someone quipped, "If you think poverty does terrible things to people, you should see what wealth can do." It is true. Ask Bernie Madoff or Elizabeth Holmes, Leona Helmsley or, in Texas, any former Enron employee.

The chief spiritual dilemma of our age is materialism—not just in its economic sense, but also in its philosophical sense. We have taught succeeding generations that the real things, the most valuable things, the things we should want and trust, are those things that can be measured, touched, tasted, smelled, bought, owned, sold, acquired.

I have no intention to initiate some sophomoric guilt trip about our third cars and smart TVs. Conversations about generosity should center on joy and thanksgiving, not guilt and shame. Besides, the Bible never says that money—or the things it buys—is bad or evil or wrong. Presbyterians in particular have decried a world denying asceticism as an offense to the incarnation. "God was in Christ reconciling the world unto himself" (2 Cor. 5:19 KJV). The world. The cosmos. All of the created order has been redeemed by God, and now, even now God is hard at work bringing it to serve God's purposes.

Our theological patron, John Calvin, did not bark against wealth per se; instead, he said that the idolatry lay not in a thing itself, but in our craving for it, and in the compromises we are willing to make in order to satiate our cravings. Woodrow Wilson, a Presbyterian minister's son, then a young man living in Atlanta, wrote sarcastically that in that city, "the chief end of man is certainly to make money, and money cannot be made except by the most vulgar methods."[2]

In his caution concerning our cravings Calvin was merely echoing Scripture, of course. Cravings can lead us astray, blind us, distort our souls and skew our priorities. The third car and large home can be acceptable things. Yet they often bring a spiritual cost beyond their sales tag. Richard Foster summarizes the cost like this:

Because we lack a divine Center our need for security has led us into an insane attachment to things. We really must understand that the lust for affluence in contemporary society is psychotic. It is psychotic because it has completely lost touch with reality. We crave things we neither need nor enjoy. . . . . It is time we awaken to the fact that conformity to a sick society is to be sick."[3]

Long ago a congregation I served hosted a young Honduran woman for a year through the denomination's Reconciliation in Mission program. The program brought Central Americans to live and work within North American congregations. It bridged gaps, built friendships, shattered stereotypes and misperceptions. I asked her just before she went home what she would tell her home congregation about her American hosts. She said, "I will tell them that this is a wonderful church full of kind people, and that your task is to learn what to do with all your things."

Here is the saddest and most destructive part of this complex matrix we call materialism. Materialism dares to posit an audacious and alternative explanation of what human beings are for. In this alternative myth, people are worth the resources we command. A person's value is determined by the clothes he wears, the car she drives, the house they inhabit, the accounts they accumulate.

Christians know that people are not worth what we acquire. Christians know that human beings are infinitely valuable because we breathe. Children of God. Made in the image of God. Which is straight from the Bible—the creation story.

It is tempting to think that because the creation story opens the first pages of the Bible, it was written earliest. It was not. It was written fairly late in the Old Testament period. It was written by Jewish priests serving an exile community in ancient Babylon. They were reminding God's people who they were, and whose. And they were doing so to counter the Babylonian creation myth that held that there are multiple gods, and that these gods created human beings as slaves. Slaves!

So these faithful, exilic priests wrote a beautiful piece of worship liturgy to remind God's people who they were and what God wants. That creation story says it all. "And it was good. And it was very good." The creation is good! We are good.

Slaves? Nonsense. We are not slaves. We are partners. Friends. God sets us amidst abundance in order that you might live together in safety, plenty, and joy.

And what do we do? We force into America's classrooms the compulsion to teach our children that this creation liturgy is a scientific explanation of the creation process even while we perpetuate a rival materialist mentality that places people back into slavery. Slavery to the myth of materialism. Slavery to the idea that one's value is measured by what one owns. Slavery to the idea that what one owns, one deserves.

Calvinism is complex and multifaceted, but I have some-times thought it reducible to a single idea: none of us deserves a thing, thanks be to God. Our obsession with getting what we deserve is misplaced.

This is, finally, the problem with prosperity. Prosperity produces presumption. We presume that what we have, we have earned. We presume that what we have earned, we deserve. Into this pit of presumption, the gospel bellows a stern warning: life is not about getting what we deserve. It is instead about a God so loving that God has given the entire world. We do not get what we deserve. We get what God gives. God gives and gives and gives. God cannot help it. That is who God is.

Our only question, then, is what are we going to do to say thank you? How are we going to live? How will we move and breathe and have our being in such a way to thank and honor a God who makes such life abundant possible?

This is why a congregation's generosity program is about so much more than meeting the church's budget. There is nothing more singularly liberating in this culture, our culture, than to give something up, to sacrifice, and then to discover contentment in doing so. In a cultural climate that teaches us to cling, it is truly a subversive act to release. It is countercultural. It is an act of complete intellectual and spiritual rebellion to say, "No, I will not hold this to myself. I will instead sacrifice it for a larger purpose. I will set it aside for a more holy use."

This is a central message of the gospel and should therefore be the centerpiece of our teaching about generosity. A mature and fully blossomed theology of generosity is the exuberant conversation within which we step toe-to-toe with the idolatries of the age and declare with a loud and clear and defiant voice, "I am not your slave! I am a child of God. I have been sealed by the Holy Spirit and marked as Christ's forever. Nothing you say or do can ever make that not true."

Why did God command Abraham to sacrifice Isaac when Isaac was twelve? Because if God had waited until Isaac was thirteen, it would not have been a sacrifice.

My teenage children did not like this joke. By the time they hit thirteen, they had heard this joke many times, but they had heard this litany much more often. "You are a child of God, sealed by the Holy Spirit, and marked as Christ's forever. Nothing anyone ever says or does can make that not true."

When they were children, I tried to repeat this litany to them every single day. I would trace the sign of the cross on their foreheads and repeat the litany—repeat it ad nauseam, they would add. One of my children, then about seven, looked up at me one day as I started the litany. "You are a child of God," I began.

"I know, I know," she interrupted, rolling her eyes, "sealed by the Holy Spirit," she mimicked. But she knew the litany, the entire litany, all of it.

This liturgy describes the essence of their identity. I said it hoping to provide an alternative to the competing messages kids receive about who they are and why they matter. Like all teenagers, these rival identities no doubt poked at them and prodded, in the classroom, on the ballpark, in the back seat, and at the shopping mall. When those rival identities were singing their siren songs, I wanted my children to lapse almost involuntarily into this mantra, "You are a child of God, sealed by the Holy Spirit, marked as Christ's forever. Nothing anyone ever says or does can make that not true."

No matter the size of your home. No matter the gloss of your car. Little difference about the cut of your clothes, the complexity of your 1040, the prestige of your position. Children of God. Marked. Sealed. Forever.

If churches teach this—if we believe this!—there will annually be held around our congregations' many kitchen tables a joyous declaration of independence as people engage the simple act of completing their pledge cards. To view your generosity ministries as an opportunity for anything less is to forego the most powerful conversation you might ever have. And for a pastor to hesitate to preach this liberating message with confidence and power is nothing short of professional malpractice.

That is why I believe that generosity is the antidote to the chief idols of the age, namely, consumerism, materialism, and acquisition.

Chapter 8

. . . TO SERVE AS
SPIRITUAL DISCIPLINE

GENEROSITY IS AN ANCIENT SPIRITUAL DISCIPLINE. DISCIPLINED
and intentional generosity is foundational. It is the bedrock
of other time-tested and ancestor-approved spiritual practices.

My oldest brother is an Episcopal priest. Go figure. As a
student at McCormick Seminary, a Presbyterian seminary, he
went to the Soviet Union with other Presbyterian seminarians.
On their way home, they visited Geneva. While there Doug
wandered into a small Anglican worship service and had a
conversion experience. He loved the mystical implications of
the sacrament. He loved the mystery of the liturgy. What a
wonderful irony: a Presbyterian minister's son goes to Calvin's
city and becomes an Episcopalian.

Doug brought to our family of starched collar, multigen-
erational Presbyterians a deep appreciation for spirituality.
He taught me centering prayer. He invited me to try yoga.
Doug encouraged me to try fasting. He reminded me of

Calvin's sacramental theology, which opens so much more room for mystery than most Presbyterian congregations today recognize.

My brother's contributions to our family's faith practices are emblematic of a much larger integration happening across the American church. Not that long ago people were born and died in a single faith tradition, but gone are the days when one's spiritual style and understandings are limited to a single stream of denominational Christianity. Commitments to historic denominations and their traditions are dying quickly. The comparatively clean distinctions of yesteryear have given way to fuzzy boundaries and self-styled syncretism.

Now, we enter postmodernity. The intellectual and theological assumptions of the past half millennia are up for grabs. Technology is meshing and fusing both thought and custom. On the secular front, the world is flat, as Tom Friedman has it.[1] Ecclesiastically, Phyllis Tickle likened the church's current state of affairs to a five-hundred-year garage sale.[2] In my own experience, older members of every congregation I have served have voiced their observations in two simple and sequential sentences. First, "Where have the young people gone?" Then, if young people dared to return, they have bellowed, "They want to do *what?*"

Now, in this bohemian, eclectic, post-denominational and postmodern world, the measure of Christian ritual and practice has less to do with history or denominational loyalty than it does with utility, with usefulness. The litmus test for faith practices is no longer, Is it Presbyterian, or Methodist, or Catholic, or even Christian? The measure for inclusion of a particular ritual is, Does it work? Is it effective? Does it feed my soul and nourish the world?

Hence, stodgy old congregations are trying all sorts of new (to them) things, from yoga to Tai Chi, from paschal candles to labyrinths, from incense to meditation. None of these things is new, however. Each is quite old. Their use then seems a backwards leaping, jumping back hundreds of years, leaping beyond the birth of the American church, past the Reformation, backwards still. People are clamoring for authentic practices that deepen their faith and sharpen their senses for God.

My rogue Episcopalian brother mirrors for me and my family the deepening realization among many that we need not be bound by the habits and convictions of the last two generations, or three, or eight. In the soil of Christian practice there are seeds planted long ago simply awaiting our attention and gentle nourishment. I did not have to leave mainline Protestant practice to embrace a deep practice of disciplined spirituality. There is a practical, ancient, and faithful way to reverently engage the worlds of spirit and matter, mainline Protestant style. Consider yet again Matthew's sixth chapter.

The chapter begins, "Beware of practicing your piety before others in order to be seen by them. . . . So whenever you give alms, do not sound a trumpet before you, as the hypocrites do" (Matt. 6:1–2a). The passage continues to praise private and authentic religious practice and to condemn inauthentic and showy religious practice. "Whenever you give alms," it begins. "And whenever you pray," it continues. "And whenever you fast," it carries on.

When you give alms. When you pray. When you fast. In that order. Jesus takes the tripod of Jewish piety and puts it in a specific order, a particular sequence. Give. Pray. Fast.

Lest you think that the Matthean ordering is happenstance, that this preacher is making too much of almsgiving just happening to be the first mentioned, consider this: Jesus ends this pericope with that juiciest of stewardship observations: "Where your treasure is, there your heart will be also" (v. 21). Jesus begins this teaching with money and he concludes this teaching with money. "When you give alms . . . where your treasure is, there your heart will be also."

Which comes first: caring, or sharing? Which follows which: our money, or our hearts?

I have already suggested that sharing often precedes caring. As further illustration, the conflict resolves itself when we remember one simple compelling fact. Jesus' first passion was not institutions. It was not organizations. It was people. He was passionately committed to drawing people closer to God, connecting people to God, illustrating to people what a God-centered life actually looks like. Every behavior he modeled was intended to give deep life to human beings. Every behavior he condemned was countered because it kept deep life hidden from view. Every meal he shared, every parable he taught, every miracle he performed, every blessing he gave, Jesus was single-mindedly in love with people. What a dreamer.

So when it came to the subject of money—and Jesus talked a lot about money—he was not first interested in funding the temple's budget. Jesus was not and Jesus is not first interested in institutional health, in institutional budgets, in institutional perpetuation. Jesus was and remains most invested in the spiritual welfare of people.

He also assumed that those who sought a God-centered life would be generous. He assumed that those who followed him would give. "*When* you give," he said, not "*if* you give."

And yet Jesus was not anti-institutional. He did not command the destruction of the temple. He did not condemn what we would now call organized religion. Instead, he came to challenge organized religion, to revitalize organized religion, to revolutionize organized religion and to make it authentic. Jesus brought Galilee to Jerusalem. He longed for the religious institution of his day to be likewise invested in practices that bring people to deep life.

That is why healthy congregations and their leaders do not shy away from talking about money, shrink back from talking about giving. Jesus is crystal clear on the subject. Giving is good for us. Sharing is part of our spiritual growth and health. Generosity is a spiritual virtue. First, we share. Then we care. Our job then, as fellow travelers, is to encourage and to inspire one another to become more generous. This is where we start, with motivating one another to share.

There is a second part, however. The not-for-profit world offers a helpful reminder that what we do with our shared gifts really matters. In an anti-institutional age, the institutional church must demonstrate authentic generosity if it is to encourage its members to practice the same. If it matters that individual people and families share, it matters also that the church shares. Both are necessary. Both are inspiring.

Any glance at your church's budget gives as clear an insight into your congregational values as any glimpse at your personal checkbook reveals what you most care about. That was the old axiom, you know. If you want to understand your values, study your checkbook. Or your credit card statement. Either way, the point remains. Jesus says that our hearts follow our money. Where we spend our money, how we save our money, where we share our money, all of it combines as honest testimony to our values. It is more revealing than most any other evaluation. Jesus describes us very well. If we want to know ourselves, take a look at our expenditures.

As for congregations, we are called to do specific things. We worship. We study. We baptize the young, we marry those in love, and we bury the dead. We care for the ill. We accompany the lonely. We challenge the complacent. We select, then train, then follow those whom God calls to leadership. We model the possibilities of subversive reconciliation and sacrificial love, or at least we try to. We fertilize community gardens and watch the thermostat settings. We recycle. Atop it all, we reach out to the community and to the world because, as presumptuous as it sounds, we actually believe ourselves to be God's partners in the restoration of the world.

For those who want first to be convinced that the institution asking for their money can be trusted to spend it wisely, the church remains the best game in town. We do good things with God's money.

And yet Jesus' teaching—that first we share, then we care—is not only descriptive. It not only describes us. It is also prescriptive. Jesus is telling us what to do, is prescribing behavior that is good for us, behavior that brings us into deeper life. How we share our money is the spiritual compass. It points us to what matters most to us.

And, if reviewing our credit card statement reveals what matters to us, the converse is also true. We may decide what we want to matter most to us and then share with it. Our generosity can take aim at our intended values. Our sharing can point us in divinity's direction.

Marvin and Veva Byrd were long ago church members, and dear friends and mentors to me. Their remarkable story convinced me early and deeply about the importance of pointing my generosity at that about which I hoped to care.

They grew up in rural Illinois. Marvin fought in World War II, in Europe. He crossed the English Channel on D-Day plus one. His boat was hit and sunk and Marvin spent the night in the cold water. Veva did not know for months that he had survived. When he returned from Europe, the young couple had a dilemma. Marvin was asthmatic, and that would not do for an Illinois dirt farmer. So they moved. Sight unseen they took their young family to the blue skies and clean air of Roswell, New Mexico. Marvin got a job at the local hardware store.

They pledged to their church. They didn't merely pledge, either; they tithed a full ten percent of Marvin's salary. They were not haughty about it, but matter of fact. They were not legalistic, either. It was a joyous promise, a pledge of ten percent of Marvin's pretax income to the work their church was doing.

Then Marvin lost his job.

They told me this story years later, and I, across the kitchen table, a twenty-something pastor, knew exactly what was coming. They were going to tell me that sometimes, things happen. Context changes our covenants. There are circumstances, they were going to explain, which must amend the most noble of intentions.

Marvin continued. "I lost my job, and we kept that pledge." Three young boys. Unemployed. Half a nation from home with no backup plan, no family support system. All they had was the church of Jesus Christ. They kept that pledge.

Marvin is gone now. Veva, too. I can still see them in my mind's eye, Marvin serving food at Lend-a-Hand, a soup kitchen they helped organize. Veva is there, too, side by side, and also in her living room, perched in the La-Z-Boy, knitting blankets for needy newborns. Early in their adulthoods they had pointed their resources directly towards that about which they most wished to care: love, grace, mission, church. It worked. Veva and Marvin Byrd were generous to their cores, or perhaps more accurately, from their cores. Their years of intentional generosity had been spiritually transformational.

First we share. Then we care. We aim our lives with how we give.

If brother Doug has taught me anything about spirituality, it is that spirituality takes practice. And practice requires discipline. It is in the regular doing of a thing that we fully comprehend the reason for doing it. And with no spiritual discipline is this more true than with the spiritual discipline of sharing. To produce spiritual fruit, spiritual disciplines inspire, well, *discipline*. In this time when so many in our pews are clamoring to learn ancient spiritual disciplines, longing to learn the time-tested rituals of faith, we may confidently offer them the lessons of our spiritual ancestors. Prayer. Worship. Service. Fasting. Bible study. And yes, sharing—intentional, disciplined, sacrificial sharing.

To those daring postmodernists still willing to give our tradition-bound congregations a chance, we have for them the wisdom of the ages, the rock-steady examples of generations upon generations who took up specific spiritual habits and learned in their practice about nothing less than the nature of God. Disciplined generosity is a spiritual kick start, a portal for deep and authentic religious growth.

There is another note here, too, about the sequence of giving. Our grandparents and great grandparents were taught that giving came first. They gave off the top of their incomes and lived off what was left. In the offertory section of the worship bulletin, these days most bulletins read, "The Giving of *Our* Tithes and Offerings." Years ago, the nomenclature was different. It said, "The Giving of *God's* Tithes and Our Offerings." That seems a subtle distinction. It is not. Seventy-five years ago, American Christians were conscious of the idea that 10 percent of their incomes belonged to God. A tithe was simply returning to God what already belongs to God. A tithe comes from duty. An offering comes from joy. I will hand it to you that years ago, most church members did not actually tithe ten percent of their income. Still, this linguistic shift signals a seismic reordering in everyday theology. To whom, exactly, does that 10 percent belong?

Somewhere in the 1950s, I am guessing, a new term crept into our economic vocabulary: discretionary income. Most people then hardly knew what it meant. Discretionary income is what remains after the bills are paid. Emerging from the Depression, most Americans simply got by, or better yet they got by simply.

Somehow, someway, we have come to think of generosity as discretionary. After we have paid the bills, after we have had some fun, then, maybe, perhaps we will consider sharing, but only if an organization can convince us that it will spend our money precisely as it promises to, and if we care about the organization's mission, and if the organization can connect us emotionally to the recipients of our pecuniary prowess. That is three ifs on the other side of two maybes. If our hearts are where our treasure is, our hearts have become adept at practicing discretion. We have discreetly talked ourselves out of the conviction that Christian generosity is a spiritual joy.

Generosity—giving, sacrificing, risking, trusting, sharing—generosity describes a spiritual discipline whose committed practice emboldens our trust in the One who owns our abundance. We are to give because it is good for us.

That is why I believe that generosity is chief among the ancient spiritual disciplines.

Chapter 9

. . . TO PROVIDE THE BELIEVER'S CALL

SEVENTY-FIVE YEARS AGO, THE FINANCIAL SERVICES INDUSTRY pulled off a far-reaching linguistic sleight of hand. Banks created a card whereby an account holder could purchase merchandise to be paid for at some later time. Banks called this instrument a credit card because, from the institution's perspective, it extended a line of credit to the customer. In due time banks offered an additional card, this one allowing an account holder to instantly withdraw from an account into which she had previously deposited her money. This card was named a debit card.

The naming of these devices of exchange—credit accounts and debit accounts—was not done dishonestly. It was not corporate skullduggery. Banks simply named the devices from their own perspective.

Still, if identified from the customer's perspective, these cards would be identified precisely the other way around. A credit card could easily be considered an account into which the customer has previously made deposits and therefore currently holds a credit. Conversely, when a customer borrows money to make a purchase, he could just as easily consider the transaction a debit, because, without money already deposited to cover the expense, from his point of view, he actually makes a debit that must be repaid. The very terms credit and debit, as in all terms describing transactions, depend on one's point of view.

The church faces an equally interesting choice in its language regarding contributions. Congregations send a subtle but powerful message when they *take collections* versus *receive offerings*. Taking a collection is to appropriate something of value from another to benefit oneself. Receiving an offering is to accept a gift willingly given by another to advance shared goals. The language congregations choose is more than word choice; it is a matter of the heart. The decision reveals about whom the congregation is most interested—the institution, or the individuals who together constitute the institution.

Far too many congregations take collections. This explains the creeping suspicion among many Christians that congregations are more possessed by institutional self-perpetuation than they are interested in the spiritual welfare of their members. We live in an anti-institutional nation in a particularly anti-institutional age. Christian leaders must admit and confront this cynicism.

This chestnut humorously illustrates the suspicion.

A woman is struck by a bus on a busy street. She lies on the sidewalk, seriously injured. A crowd gathers. "A priest!" she gasps, "Somebody get me a priest!"

A policeman scans the crowd and yells, "A priest, please. Hurry!"

Out of the crowd steps a little Jewish man at least 80 years old. "Officer," says the man, "I'm not a priest. I'm not even a Christian. But for 50 years now, I have lived behind the

Catholic parish on First Avenue, and every night I overhear their services. I can recall much of what I have heard, and maybe I can be of some comfort to this woman."

The policeman agrees and clears the crowd so the Jewish do-gooder can kneel next to the injured woman. He bends down, leaning close to the prostrate woman, takes her hand gently into his own, and looking compassionately into her eyes says in a calming, solemn voice: "B-4. I-19. N-38. G-54. O-72."

Protestants are hardly free from such suspicion, either. I have started many a stewardship sermon with this self-critical story just to assuage the congregation's latent fear that the preacher is about to manipulate its members out of their hard-earned money.

For those confident that any congregational conversation on generosity is really the church's selfish effort to extract dollars for its own benefit, nothing disarms more quickly than humor. I am a preacher, not a comedian. Still, a stewardship sermon without humor is a carpenter's toolbox without a hammer.

Here is another joke meant to name the suspicion that the church simply wants our hard-earned money.

Two men are shipwrecked on a desert island. The first one paces the hot sand. "We're going to die," he repeats over and again. "We're shipwrecked with no food, no fresh water, and no way off and no way out."

The second man relaxes beneath a palm tree, his head comfortable in pillowed hands. "We have nothing to worry about," he says. "I make $100,000 a week," he brags.

Incredulous, the first man responds, "What good will your money do us here? There is nothing to buy. Nothing to sell. Nothing to consume. What difference can your wealth possibly make here?"

The second man replies, "I make $100,000 a week, and I tithe. My pastor will find us."

That story is guaranteed to raise a smile. And, truth told, the punchline could easily substitute the Stewardship Committee for the pastor. No matter who comes looking for the stranded tither, the laughter springs from a shared experience and a common suspicion that when it comes to generosity discussions, the church is passionately interested in meeting its budget.

And the church budget matters. The church's mission in the world is vital and distinct. The church plays a redemptive role in the lives of individuals, communities, and nations.

Still, it is likewise uncomfortably true that too many congregations take collections rather than receive offerings. Presently, much of our stewardship conversation begins with the inherited, threadbare, habitual assumption that the entire endeavor has primarily to do with funding the church's mission. In this day of shrinking membership and low institutional self-esteem, we are sending many of our members away, turned off by the whole exercise, their pristine checkbooks—or their un-swiped credit cards—in hand. We present the case for generosity as if the individual has no place in it other than contributing toward the church's need. How many church newsletter stewardship articles begin with a moan and end with a whimper? In between is a detailed report about the shrinking budget, the aging building, the underpaid staff. This is hardly the stuff of expansive joy and redemptive hope.

Our time in history has bequeathed younger Americans with a pronounced skepticism of public institutions. For middle-aged and younger American Christians, the mantra seems to be, wherever two or more are gathered, do not trust them. Many of our church members have finely tuned, permanently engaged hogwash meters. When we hear hogwash, we know it. And nothing pegs our meters to ten faster than an institutional authority figure more interested in the church's budget than in the cumulative spiritual well-being of those who contribute to it.

If you are motivated to think about generosity only because your congregation is in financial turmoil and you are wondering how to increase giving to pay the light bill, fair enough. But take note: if that is your theological pitch, you will remain in the dark.

Jesus' followers need to speak first of joy, and grace, and God, and individual spiritual discipline and benefit. The generosity conversation must burst forth in an exuberant, excited, doxological proclamation that the God who set us in the abundant garden refuses to turn God's back on us. Or close God's hand. Our stewardship context is about stepping into the generous heart of God where we might learn to be likewise generous.

The good news is that there is a much more joyous—and far less anxious—motivation for talking about generosity than the need to subscribe the church budget. Generosity is most powerful, most transformational, when it is inspired by the individual's joyous and eager response to God. Both the church and the individual matter. Nonetheless, the generosity conversation must first, now, begin with the benefit to the believer of conscious, delighted, and disciplined generosity. Our generosity is a means by which we grow more nearly into the image of Jesus Christ.

If we believe this, if we can somehow rise from our institutional preoccupations, our congregational generosity efforts will not begin with our lamentations about what the church could do *if only*. They will begin with grace-full declarations about the beauties of emulating our selfless God. If we are more interested in the well-being of our fellow disciples, and if we believe that being generous is good for them—good for us—we will let go of the idea that we are the church's fundraisers. We will speak of joy. We will sing of generosity. We will dance in abundance. We will share mercy and blessing, and we will choose to be people of charity and hope.

Part III

Speaking of Money

I lift my voice and pray:
May the lights in The Land of Plenty
Shine on the truth some day.

—Leonard Cohen, "The Land of Plenty," 2001

CONGREGATIONS, CHRISTIANS, AND MANY PASTORS STAMMER through the generosity conversation because we are so discomfited by money-talk. Oh, the pastor might preach a single stewardship sermon each year, yet I've heard many stewardship sermons so watered down to prevent offense that what was left were a couple of lightweight illustrations in search of a theological point. Hence, other than the bespectacled analysis of the distributed budget, money is rarely mentioned in many churches.

It's as if money is so profane that its embarrassed mention might somehow sully more spiritual and holy topics. Or conversely, and even worse, might it be that we have made money so holy that like Jews refusing to pronounce or even write the sacred name of God (YHWH), money is too holy to voice? Either way, such silence is ear-piercing. If the Bible is the story of God's unrelenting, cumulative generosities, and if by becoming generous we emulate God's most fundamental characteristic, we would do well to shout about it from the church steeple!

Before my health failed, I spoke on generosity often and broadly enough to reach gold status with my frequent flyer program. I spoke to groups large and small, congregations and conferences, judicatory meetings and retreats. The invitations baffled me. I wasn't saying anything outside of Christian common sense but was often told that while that may have been true, there were few speakers saying such things, which only puzzled me further.

In all my travels, no experience more shaped me than a judicatory meeting I addressed. This experience changed my thinking about mainline Christianity's willingness to talk about money. More, really; this experienced changed *me*.

When you regularly speak to crowds of strangers on touchy topics, you collect exercises designed to get the conversations going—icebreakers, if you will. A very icy wall keeps most mainliners from money talk, and that includes most pastors.

For this meeting I relied on the trusted M&M's opener. Each participant entered the meeting room to discover a mini packet of M&M's chocolates on the tables, one pack per person. I explained that the colors of the M&M's—red, yellow, blue, orange, or green—matched the colored-coded questions on a slide I next projected on a screen. The goal was to choose an M&M, answer a question matching its color, eat the M&M, and pass the turn to another person, until each person had answered at least three questions. The questions were simple, straightforward, at least the first part of them, but the questions toward the bottom became more personal, more revealing, more daring. The icebreaker allows each person to participate at whatever level of vulnerability they prefer.

On this particular day, the bottom questions were incredibly risky. In fact, I didn't intend for anyone to answer them. I would never have asked such questions in a group of mainline Protestants. I added them for effect only, to illustrate that few congregations speak freely about money. To signal that I didn't intend for anyone to answer the questions, I color-coded them black. Afterall, there are no black M&M's. They aren't made. Participants would soon catch on that they had no black M&M's and therefore wouldn't have to worry about answering the questions. Simply by putting the questions in writing, I would illustrate our lockjawed assumptions against speaking of such things.

Here are the black questions I asked that day: How much money did you make last year, and how much did you give to the church?

I hadn't wanted to stuff M&M's mini packs into my suitcase for this October event, so I asked my host to purchase and have them ready. They did. After reviewing each question on my projected list, I finally triggered my trap; I asked those delightful, innocent, trusting people to open their M&M's packets and to spread a few candies out before them. Who would be the first to yell out that there are no black M&M's?

Did you know that Mars Wrigley Confectionery Inc. makes special, once-a-year, Halloween-edition M&M's packs that include black M&M's? I did not.

Realizing my error, I stumbled through an embarrassed apology. I would never have asked such questions had I realized that there are, in fact, black M&M's, I said. I sputtered through a word salad of self-conscious excuses and finally asked the crowd's forgiveness for my unintended impertinence. It was hilarious, we all seemed to agree, but accidental. No one need worry about answering the question.

As I stopped talking, an old woman stood at the back of the room. An awkward silence descended. All heads turned to her. Then, she arched her back and in a strong and confident voice, she answered the questions. She blurted out both her income and her pledge, publicly, in front of God and everybody. Then a thirty-something man, a schoolteacher, rose to his feet, and he, too, answered the question. And on it went.

This, this was *church*. The Spirit had snookered me! Well beyond my planning, a community of strangers blundered into an experience of transcendent joy. There was no one-upmanship. There was no arrogance. There were only humble stewards celebrating together that God had inspired them to generosity.

Was that experience possible because most of those people didn't know one another, didn't worship in the same congregation? Or might such openness and vulnerability be possible within a congregation?

That M&M's moment has convinced me that congregations—pastors, leaders, and parishioners—are capable of far
deeper thought and conversation about money than we have
given ourselves credit for being. And this is certain—unleashing generosity requires open conversation, and conversation
requires open spirits and open minds.

The final section of our book, then, the "Now What,"
concerns this—unleashing passion for speaking openly about
money, at the kitchen table, in congregational meeting rooms,
and in the sanctuary.

And this is also certain—such openness cannot be reached
without the pastor's leadership and example. Before the pastor
may speak bravely, openly with congregational leaders, and
from the pulpit, the pastor must initiate a thorough and vulnerable conversation with her authentic self.

Chapter 10

THE PASTOR'S
INTERNAL DIALOGUE

THE MODERN PASTOR IS AMONG THE LAST PROFESSIONAL GENERAL-
ists. While most professions tend to ever greater specialization,
pastors, especially those serving smaller membership congregations, must be reasonably good at many things: preaching,
pastoral care, counseling, writing, editing, staff management,
strategic planning, meeting planning and moderating—and
the list goes on. The job description also includes inspiring
generosity, includes leading congregational generosity efforts,
but, truth told, leading the generosity conversation is for many
pastors among our least favorite professional tasks. Least
favorite often equals most dreaded.

How could it be different? Given our theology of ordina-
tion, most Protestant pastors think of ourselves first as disciples, second as pastors of the church of Jesus Christ, third
as pastors of a particular denomination, and only finally as
pastors of single Christian communities. Our essence is our
humanity, rooted in God's creativity, and our commitment is

to God through the incarnate Word. Our call is to serve Jesus Christ within Christ's church, and God seems time and again to call pastors who deeply love people—caring for them, worshiping amongst them, working with them to bear witness to and to model God's coming reign. Ministry is something we *do*, not something we *are*; pastors want to do ministry that benefits people and their communities.

Discussing money is not, then, a first-tier call. Has any pastor felt called to ministry longing that someday she will preach stewardship sermons? Ever? Who began ministry with a burning desire to author a stewardship brochure?

I've spent a great deal of time with pastors over the last three decades, much of it discussing generosity, stewardship programs, and the church's financial context. At stewardship conferences, usually in the evening, after the group dinner when clergy cluster into self-sorted conversation groups, finally, truths emerge. Walls crumble. Vulnerabilities surface. Confessions tumble forth.

Ask such a group to explore its reticence to speak openly about money and the first explanations tend to be biblical. Almost invariably, pastors begin quoting Jesus: "When you give alms, do not let your left hand know what your right hand is doing, so that your alms may be done in secret; and your Father who sees in secret will reward you" (Matt. 6:3–4). You can't mention these verses without tending the verses nearby, so the conversation swings to the larger context of Matthew 6 in which Jesus also admonishes the disciples to pray behind closed doors, privately. Yet, we all pray publicly. Regularly. It's literally in our job descriptions. Jesus recommends privacy not only for almsgiving and prayer, but also for fasting, a spiritual practice long ago redefined if not jettisoned altogether by most American Protestants. Is it honest to pick or pluck texts so clearly adjacent to one another?

Other than Matthew 6, does Jesus otherwise recommend a tongue-tied privacy about giving? Ultimately, no pastor argues for long that we shouldn't talk about money because Jesus didn't. Read the gospels. By some counts Jesus talks more about money than any subject other than the kingdom of God.

Paul isn't helpful, either, to those seeking cover for a biblical gag order on financial conversation in the church. Think of his praise for the churches of Macedonia and their generosity in 2 Corinthians 8. Paul quite clearly goads the Corinthians to greater giving with the Macedonian example—all the more noteworthy as first century Macedonia was a poor city and yet a model of generosity, while Corinth was a rich city—and this is only one place in which he speaks so openly about the church's need and the necessity of sharing resources.

The evening grows late and still the conversation continues for the brave few. Following a thorough biblical review, it drifts next to historic comparisons. Much has changed in 2,000 years. The solutions were different, the thinking goes, in a culture practicing ritualistic sacrifice amidst an economy of subsistence agriculture and nascent labor specialization. Today, with a modern tax system and a social safety net, the church's role is radically different. We each contribute to the social safety net—aimed at biblical orphans and widows, and much more—whether we want to or not. Observing this, this conversation generally winds itself into a fury, essentially detailing all the ways Christians contribute to shared solutions outside the church, including the wonderful work done by so many not-for-profits, all of which might warrant an even less generous hand for the church. After all, if other organizations are filling needs the church used to meet, perhaps it is ethical to reduce our giving to the church. I've marveled at the intellectual gymnastics that follow as even pastors find reasons that the biblical tithe is too high an expectation. Say what you will about the tithe, but Jesus would say that the biblical tithe is the floor of our generosity, not the ceiling. (We'll think about the tithe in the next chapter.)

Finally, our late-night conversations whittle our reasoning to the bone, and most pastors reluctantly conclude that our hesitance on these matters has less to do with biblical interpretation or historic comparisons than it has to do with us, with our personal histories, fears, and feelings.

Well, of course it does. And it does for everyone.

Pastors graduate with expensive seminary degrees denominations require for jobs they are largely unable to provide. Next, newly ordained pastors often enter ministry serving small membership congregations or as associate pastors in larger membership congregations, commonly drawing meager wages in either situation, yet they carry undergraduate and seminary debt that will strain their economic resources for at least the first decade of their ministries. (Is it irreverent to observe that at least in this sense, even the original disciples had the edge? Jesus sent them out two by two, with "nothing for their journey except a staff; no bread, no bag, no money in their belts" (Mark 6:8). That's risky, but at least they didn't start the journey with debt!)

Nonetheless, these passionate, committed servants step into the stewardship pulpit often among their congregation's top givers, though they are not among the congregation's top earners. To top it off, many church members carry an unspoken (subconscious?) expectation that their pastor will live the same lifestyle they do—buy a home in a similar neighborhood, drive a comparable car, dress equally professionally—though a pastor's pay rarely provides for such. Then, pastors preach to skeptical, anxious worshipers, at least some of whom hear in a vision for increased giving nothing but an agenda for institutional self-preservation, or worse, they hear the self-interested pastor advocating for a raise. Add to these realities that many pastors are much better with people than we are with balance sheets, better with relationships than with checkbooks, and it is easy to see why at least some pastors approach the generosity conversation with mumbling under-confidence and infectious personal discomfort.

What irony: no congregation can ultimately have a successful generosity ministry without the pastor's full-throated support and example, yet many pastors feel ill-equipped to lead it. In the wealthiest land the world has ever known, among the richest disciples the Christian church has ever included, how to share God's resources is among the most important conversations the American church will lead. Bluntly, pastors must simply conjure the courage to guide the generosity conversation. Or it will never happen. And the conversation has never been more important.

There are hurdles on the track. Common hurdles. Tall hurdles. Just imagine things from a pastor's perspective in any one of the following scenarios.

You want to trust that God provides, but in recent years it's been harder to count on. When you finally paid the last of your education debt, you assumed your budget would discover some breathing room, but then your family had a medical emergency and the air conditioner compressor failed. Now you're back where you began. The stewardship committee is gearing up for the fall campaign and asks you and the congregation's board to increase your annual pledges by ten percent. You feel frightened, embarrassed, and paralyzed. How can you preach convincingly about God's generosity when you're not personally confident that you have enough to share?

Or what of this scenario? You and your family have long been generous with the church and your favorite charities, giving well above even a ten percent tithe. You have sacrificed luxuries and experiences along the way, but still, your kids seem to appreciate your generosity example and your marriage feels all the stronger for its construction around these shared values. Normally, your generosity brings you pure joy and a humble satisfaction. Lately, though, your feelings have been more complex. This morning, as you arrived at the church, a good-natured friend and church member noticed your new shoes and quipped, "New shoes, eh? We are paying you too much!" You laugh and think little of it, but somehow it nags at you through the morning. Then, at lunch, another church member describes his family's coming vacation. The vacation will cost multiples of what he gives to the church, yet you wish him a happy trip. You feel resentful and petty, jealous and immature. You can hardly admit these feelings to yourself, much less to another person. How can you preach humbly about the joys of being generous without laying an unintended guilt trip on your congregation, or without appearing nauseatingly self-righteous, all the while masking your embarrassed resentment?

And what of this situation? You're freshly ordained and completely excited, chock-full of ideas about doing ministry in your first congregation. At your first stewardship committee meeting, the chairperson introduces the committee, then turns to you, saying, "Well, how do you want to do stewardship this year?" Your mind races back to the two seminary class lectures you heard on the topic. You have never pledged regularly to a church. You have never given much thought to a theology of generosity. You have certainly never organized and led a months-long program to focus a congregation's attention on sharing. The committee awaits your word. You feel overwhelmed, ill-prepared, and downright scared. How can you lead this effort given your inexperience, ignorance, and fear?

Another circumstance facing pastors—the post-COVID-19 challenge. Your congregation seemed comparatively healthy before the pandemic, but now, as fewer members return to church life, you wonder if COVID-19 has wrought permanent change. The voices of the congregation's periphery are now amplified and many of the regulars, who used to balance those at the edge, have not yet returned. Of those no longer worshiping with you, you aren't sure if they're gone forever, or, if they are open to returning, what might entice them home. The slightest mention of the hot button issues—race, partisan elections, abortion, cable news personalities, gun safety and control—either stops conversations cold or explodes into rancor and hurt feelings. Members are using their generosity to express frustration over the cultural divide, or maybe they have just grown disinterested. Either way, giving is down. Is it even possible to preach a joyous word on generosity into such a troubled context?

And perhaps the most troubling scenario of all: you serve a small membership congregation filled with people who are indeed proportionately generous, but most of whom strain simply to get by. You share dreams for vibrant ministry but there simply aren't the resources between you to pay for them, particularly considering that your compensation package accounts for a high percentage of the church's budget. Your members love you, and you them, and objectively you are clearly necessary for the congregation's cohesion and envisioned mission. Still, you are self-conscious about the sacrifices necessary simply to keep you on staff. How do you speak past your discomfort with a generosity teaching that will keep the dreams alive while also acknowledging the congregation's limited resource pool?

If these scenarios don't illustrate the hurdles that leave preachers stumbling and bruised, there are more: anxiety about being judged; fear of scarcity; a spouse who doesn't agree to share at the same level; embarrassment about debt; the hope that church members will never know about the messiness of your personal finances along with the nagging shame that if only you were a better money manager, you wouldn't be in this situation; resentment about working long hours for low pay, especially when jealousy or covetousness find a crack in your soul. Add to this a broad, general discomfort with the church's financial life, and the reality that as soon as the budget is shared around the meeting table, many pastors' eyes roll to the back of our heads.

It would be funny if it weren't so painful, and it would be painful if we allowed ourselves the spiritual space to experience and label the sources of our discomfort. Naming emotions, after all, confers power to those brave enough to do so. Mostly, though, we don't name those emotions. We allow such fleeting thoughts to ping our psyches without pausing to filter them theologically, or psychologically, and finally it becomes easier to carry on as we always have, each stewardship season resorting to yesterday's formulas and clichés, those same time-tortured sermons and platitudes.

Pastors, have I come anywhere near approximating your experience? Others, can you empathize with the awkward expectations pastors face?

I am arguing that generosity is God's most basic characteristic; and that practicing generosity is fundamental to religious joy; and that the pastor is singularly placed to remind the church that these things are true. But we simply must confess how difficult it is for many pastors to do so.

There is no magic wand, no panacea, no simple way to strip the complexities so that the pastor may leap unfettered into the fray. Authentic openness on these issues will require intention, trust, and time. Most important of all, before generosity can be the pastor's message, generosity must first be the pastor's teacher.

If you seek to become more generous, what's holding you back?

We live in a day, particularly post-COVID-19, when growing numbers of Americans are detaching religion from the church. In a moaning shift, many Americans see faith in highly individual terms, simultaneously deinstitutionalizing their spiritual practices. Surveys show the fast-paced growth of the "nones," people who identify with no particular religious community.[1] It is ever more common to hear people self-identify as "spiritual" but not "religious" as they shift their spiritual practices away from the practice of public ritual in pursuit of an "inner" experience of God.[2] This isn't surprising, given the cultural trends since Watergate, in which Americans have turned a jaundiced eye to government, to education, and to business. We live in a profoundly anti-institutional age. Even in the church, filled with disciples who have consciously chosen to remain there, we find a subtle tendency to bifurcate authentic Christian faith from its practice in the institutional church.

The pastor stands, then, in a very clumsy position—seeing the church's failures and hypocrisies face-to-face, yet called to preach and live a gospel of generosity. One senses, in my late-night clergy conversations, a grounded commitment to defending the church, its inadequacies duly noted, but also an unnoticed willingness to conflate Christian faith with the Christian church, as if they are one and the same. Turns out, the "spiritual" versus "religious" crowd may have something to teach us. Many pastors might conclude that our hesitance to bold generosity grows from our inner doubts about the church. I wonder if this isn't a handy distraction.

The pastor wonders, for instance, if I trust in the church's provision and risk accordingly, will there be enough left over to enjoy a reasonable standard of living? If I give sacrificially to the church, will the church stand behind me should I or my family face need? If I risk for the church, and it lets me down, what will I do? Who then would I become?

Is the pastor's resistance most basically practical—involving our relationship with the church—or is it primarily spiritual, involving our relationship with God? Try replacing church with God in each of those sentences above. If I trust in God's provision and risk accordingly, will there be enough left over to enjoy a reasonable standard of living? If I give sacrificially with God, will God stand behind me should I or my family face need? If I risk for God, and God lets me down, what will I do? Who then would I become?

At root, the pastor's basic struggle is spiritual, so perhaps our goal is to be both spiritual and religious. Perhaps the wrestling match that must be won before a pastor can practice and preach bold generosity is an internal affair, a deeply personal and spiritual matter.

So again, if you seek to become more generous, what's holding you back?

As I have analyzed what holds me back in my own life, two central biblical affirmations have freed me for generosity's journey time and again: "The earth is the LORD's and all that is in it" (Ps. 24:1a), and "The LORD is my shepherd, I shall not want" (Ps. 23:1). Do you trust these affirmations?

I am not yet as generous as I would like to be. But I am trying. What I know of generosity has come only after trying it. Generosity's truth is self-confirming. It has not always been fun, and it certainly has not always been easy. Yet, each time I and my family have stretched to share more, I have felt myself freer to talk about the experience, more willing to encourage others to try for themselves, clearer about what the Bible teaches, and infinitely more thankful for my life in Christ. Now especially, writing from a hospice bed, the embarrassment of riches flowing to me from God fills my head and heart and nothing appears to me more beautiful than sharing what God has lavished upon me. In fact, generosity has become my life's chief joy, the every-day-renewing enterprise to share resources, time, kindness, words, my deepest self.

Before generosity can be the preacher's message, it must first be the pastor's teacher.

To pastors who have wondered the things I have wondered, having difficulty imagining life on the other side of the hurdles, I can recommend only that you begin the practice of disciplined, consistent, and sacrificial generosity. As my brother Drew has it, we must practice what we preach if we are to preach what we practice. You might be yet amazed at how easy it becomes to lead others toward their own growth in generosity.

Chapter 11

THE PASTOR SPEAKS WITH CONGREGATION LEADERS

PASTORS MUST LEAD ALL CONGREGATIONAL GENEROSITY EFFORTS— and if not, set their tone quite publicly—but faithful and successful generosity ministry will include many people in its creative envisioning and execution. What pastors say to lay leaders, then, is crucial.

There are six bellwether conversations—two primarily theological, four primarily practical—to be had with a congregation's lay leadership on the journey to a holistic, joyous, and long-term generosity ministry. They are:

- What are our fundamental convictions about generosity?
- How do we charge and staff the stewardship committee?
- Should we use a system of pledges?
- Should the pastor share how much she gives?
- Should the pastor know how much others give?
- Should we teach the tithe?

The typical annual stewardship campaign usually follows this trajectory: The congregation's governing body—the session, vestry, board—projects next year's expenses. It distributes that budget along with motivational/explanatory material by any of the regular means—the congregation's website, newsletters, "minutes for mission" in worship, worship bulletin inserts, special mailings, emailings, text messages, and so on. The pastor next preaches the dreaded annual stewardship sermon on the previously announced Stewardship Sunday, which means that anyone who does not want to hear about money simply skips worship that day. Members are invited to pledge, perhaps online, and/or pledge cards are posted on the website, distributed by mail, or placed on a narthex table, or they are taken door-to-door by parishioners. Next, members return pledge cards on a designated Sunday, dedicate them in worship, and they are then tallied by the treasurer who promises that no one else will ever, ever see private financial information, excepting, of course, any paid staff who make accounting entries, mail statements, etc. The responsible governing body now makes necessary adjustments to the budget, and next year, as with shampoo, rinse and repeat.

Sound familiar? For at least three generations this model dominated American Protestantism. It bears the marks and impulses of its time: it relishes process, it is highly centralized, and it assumes at least a modicum of commitment to, and trust in, an institution. And truth told, there aren't many other options. If the church is to fund its work, and if members are to be part of its funding strategy, this system is comparatively stable.

However, this system can be reimagined and improved, and in as many ways as there are congregations to imagine local perfections. The best practical improvements will be built atop a shared theology of generosity, which is of course what this book seeks to provide. But can a book-length work be concentrated into the proverbial thirty-second elevator speech, something memorable enough that people can hear it, own it, and share it?

Yes. And its memorability resides in its sequence. American Christians are conditioned—by churches, not-for-profits, educational institutions, and so on—for institutional pitches. The presumptive sequence is almost always: explain the need and the money will come. If people care, they will share.

In the church this sequence begins with next year's budget, moves to the members' responsibility, and might finally reference God as a validation for both. Though most stewardship campaigns choose a biblical text as their organizing theme, after the theme is chosen it is rarely mentioned as anything other than perhaps an afterthought. The message is undeniable. What church members hear is that the entire endeavor has mostly to do with funding the institutional church. Why else would we begin by presenting next year's dream budget before even a mention of God and the believer?

Let us reverse the sequence.

What if the order of our thinking began with God's generosity, moved to the spiritual beauty of participating in God's generosity, and only finally described what the congregation hopes to accomplish in the coming year? In other words, imagine a stewardship season intentionally designed to pose three questions and in this order:

1. In what ways is God generous with you?
2. In what ways might you be more generous with others?
3. In what ways will our congregation be generous in the coming year?

Imagine guided conversations on these questions, led and later summarized by the pastor(s) and members of the generosity committee. Imagine these conversations held first at a meeting of the governing body; then, on a given Sunday, during every church school class from the middle school class and older; then, at choir practice, at the meetings of men's and women's groups; then, at a Zoom gathering for people who have yet to attend one of these conversations. Attention will need to be paid if everyone is to be included, particularly the aged and mobility impaired.

The beginning topic, "In what ways has God been generous with you?" is explosive. Participants compete to speak next. Most people are natural theologians given the chance to be, so "counting one's blessings" is easily directed to deeper thoughts about the nature and essence of God.

Most people begin thinking in concrete terms, thanking God for material things: houses, clothes, nourishment. Children often remain at this level of reflection, but most teens and adults begin quickly to reflect upon other, less tangible gifts. Thoughts deepen. What begins as an inventory of stuff evaporates into a reflection about the wonder of forgiveness, or the well-being that comes from having found the right romantic partner, or the memory of a time God was present amidst great hardship. There are as many ways to particularize God's generosity as there are people who have experienced it, so simply posing the question links people to an innate intuition for expansive faith expression.

"Now, tell us in what ways you might be more generous with others." Having framed God's generosity in their thinking and in their past, people move naturally toward imagining generosity expressed in their own lives. The corollaries become obvious. If God was generous with me in forgiveness, who might I forgive? If God was present with me in a difficult time, who around me is struggling and would perhaps benefit from my presence? If God's generosity calmed my insecurity fears with abundance, whose insecurity might I attempt to soothe? If God has been merciful with me, who around me craves mercy, and if God has gifted me with justice, who struggles amidst injustice? Notice here the movement between loving God with one's entirety and loving neighbor as oneself, and, as Jesus has it, "There is no other commandment greater than these" (Mark 12:31b). In fact, to the scribe who condensed religion to these two maxims, Jesus said, "You are not far from the kingdom of God" (v. 34).

Posing these questions in this order is, then, asking us to imagine our participation in the kingdom, here already, though not completely realized, not yet. And if Christ has inaugurated God's kingdom and invited our participation in it, most Christians understand and organize our efforts within the church. Hence, having pondered God's generosity and the possibilities of our personal generosity, we are primed for the follow-up question: "In what ways might our congregation be generous in the coming year?"

Now, finally, comes the time to discuss the congregation's mission and budget. Having imagined the prior generosities, we are poised to place the church's work and mission in light of questions larger than mere institutional self-preservation or the church's need to receive. We are ready for the idea that the entire generosity conversation has much less to do with what we had thought it to be about—the church's need—and much more to do with encouraging one another to grow ever more generous together, fashioning a community faithful to the values of reconciliation and redemption.

Our tithes and offerings are not organizational dues. They are God's gifts to and for the world.

God. Believer. And only then, church.

Imagine a three-part sermon series structured on this theo-logic. Picture a newsletter written and illustrated with this reasoning. Visualize an age-appropriate, congregation-wide church school curriculum, posing these questions in a three-Sunday sequence, reaching a crescendo with pledging and dedicating on the fourth Sunday, then reported upon for a full year with weekly storytelling in corporate worship about specific ministries the church is offering in and for the larger world.

This generosity campaign—complete with sermon texts and starters, newsletter content suggestions, and church school curriculum—already exists, though it is not yet published. It will not come from a denominational headquarters or printing house. There is no need to hire an expensive consulting firm—though many congregations would benefit from professional help—to begin such a program. This entire generosity campaign is waiting patiently in the faith and creative imaginations of pastors and laypeople alike, unknowingly waiting to be connected in the cause. It is best as an organic, dynamic local effort, carefully guided by a courageous pastor and a dedicated team of church members.

How do we charge and staff the generosity committee?

Allow me a word about congregations of different membership sizes. I was fortunate to have served a small, a medium, and a large membership congregation, with calls of 9 years, 8 years, and 12 years, respectively. In some ways, these congregations were strikingly different, but in ways they were likewise oddly similar. My thoughts on stewardship committees have been forged in all three contexts, and committee structures are indeed starkly different in small and large congregations.

At this printing, 72 percent of congregations in the Presbyterian Church (USA) have 150 members or less.[1] Many have fifty or less. Presbyterians are hardly alone. In fact, one study of 15,278 U.S. congregations reveals the shrinking of American congregational life. The survey found that the country has an estimated 350,000 religious congregations, and that roughly half of them see 65 or fewer people in worship on any given weekend.[2] And the survey was fielded before COVID-19.

Clearly, a congregation with 700 worshiping on Sundays will have a different committee structure than one worshiping with 65. In fact, the small membership church may well have no committees at all; its governing body may handle all decisions. In such circumstance, these following observations might still be useful. I will suggest separating committee work by function; smaller membership governing bodies might think instead of separating work by concept, that is, by being clear about the differences of planning budgets and raising money toward those budgets.

Let's begin with what a stewardship committee is not.

The stewardship committee is not the budget and finance committee. Congregations must have a committee that oversees the budgeting process, that is projecting expenditures and supervising spending. However, all too many congregations confuse and conflate this task with fundraising. They hand to a single committee both responsibilities—building a budget and inspiring generosity toward it. Building budgets and raising dollars for those budgets are related tasks, but they are different.

Saddling a single committee with *building* a budget and *meeting* that budget diminishes its ability to do either. It will either restrain its imagination regarding generosity—having met the church's budget, it will fail to imagine a larger generosity horizon for the congregation's members; or it will limit its imagination regarding the budget—merely calcifying the congregation's ministries based singularly upon last year's giving patterns. Healthy congregations need a group of leaders committed to envisioning next year's ministries and to managing the month-to-month expenditures along the way. This is a budget and finance management task and should be the responsibility of a budget and finance committee.

Likewise, healthy congregations need a group of leaders dedicated to the task of inspiring every parishioner to more generous lifestyles. Church members are encouraged to generosity with the church's mission, but a dedicated stewardship committee won't stop dreaming once the budget is met. Generosity extends well beyond the church's mission. This task belongs to the stewardship committee.

The stewardship committee is not the fundraising committee. While it is true that stewardship committees encourage monetary generosity, the committee that limits itself to raising money cannot grow toward the broader vision of raising consciousness. An exciting and comprehensive generosity vision will engage the committee's imagination around the clock, across the calendar, and regarding more than only money. What talent does each parishioner have that might be constructive to the congregation's ministry? What abilities have prepared which disciples to engage whichever of the congregation's efforts? Who has time on her hands, skill at his fingertips, and training in her past that might be helpful in the congregation's participation in God's ongoing work in the church and beyond it? As generosity is about more than sharing money, inspired stewardship committees will inspire more than financial generosity.

The stewardship committee is not the *stewardship* committee. If stewardship is more than *managing* God's possessions, but is also and especially *sharing* God's possessions, might we rename every stewardship committee in the land? What say we call it the generosity committee? (For more on the distinction between stewardship and generosity, revisit the preface.) Renaming a committee does not itself a revolution make. Still, renaming a stewardship committee as a generosity committee is one element in changing the congregational mindset of that group of leaders within every congregation charged with modeling and inspiring a more authentic practice of charity.

So what is the generosity committee for? The generosity committee's task is not first to meet the church's budget. The task is not first to raise money at all. It is to raise consciousness—consciousness of God's generosity, consciousness of God's trustworthiness, and consciousness of the remarkable possibilities of humanity's joyous and visionary responses. Members of the generosity committee understand other congregation members not as students to be convinced, but as fellow travelers along a shared path toward ever-growing generosity. The committee partners with fellow disciples in envisioning, describing, and living lifestyles of trust, joy, and openhandedness.

Maybe a generosity committee's success could be measured when church members begin leaving bigger tips at restaurants. I'm only half jesting.

My credit card company keeps an ever-watchful eye on my transactions, always on the lookout for fraud and abuse. My credit card provider emailed me, concerned about a tip I left a restaurant waiter. It read, "We hope it's because your service was exceptional. However, we wanted to check in, in case this charge needs to be reviewed." Generosity can be startling in a culture tailored to self-interest and accumulation.

Surely there are better ways to measure a generosity committee's success. And yet, the idea is basic and the point remains—a faithful and visionary generosity committee imagines on behalf of the entire congregation such trust in God, such generative possibilities, that meeting the church's annual budget is only one item on its task list. Its tasks are prophetic, comprehensive, and year-round. They include inspiring congregants to pledge and to tithe (or to work toward a tithe) and beyond. They include partnering with people as together they imagine sharing accumulated wealth after death. They include motivating members toward the construction and maintenance of an inviting and useful church facility.

And yet, the generosity committee's real fun begins when it changes and expands the congregation's attitude about money and possessions, about holding on and letting go, about lifestyle and life choices. Imagine a congregation whose Sunday school classes speak freely and comfortably about financial giving. Imagine a congregation whose children share and whose teenagers contribute and whose newlyweds pledge. Imagine a worshiping community whose participants converse openly about confronting their temptations to excessive accumulation. Imagine a church whose members are so genuinely convinced that the congregation authentically cares about their spiritual well-being and growth that God's Holy Spirit leaps them beyond their institutional skepticism and they catch an impassioned dream for the congregation's mission and ministry. Imagine the day when your congregation's ushers need deeper offering plates and when your church's board must have called meetings to explore where to share its extra funds.

These are not quixotic meanderings, illusory recollections of an overly idealized Christendom. They are the very possible dreams for any generosity committee convinced of God's provision, captured by the Spirit's hopes, and carried by the gospel conviction that "God so loved the world that God gave."

Such a generosity committee presumes at least two ingredients: the pastor's leadership, which we have discussed, and a specifically qualified membership. The generosity committee is only as strong as its members, and its members must share one central, vital, and elementary characteristic. Every member of the generosity committee must have a history of committed, intentional generosity, and also, the willingness to share with others that they have. As we have said, the truths of generosity are self-confirming. Only when we practice generosity can we understand the importance and beauty of practicing generosity. The joy, the liberation of growing in generosity, is the singular precondition for participating on a visionary generosity committee. (Note that I did not say that the committee is made up of the congregation's biggest givers. Rather, each committee member should have a history of intentional, disciplined giving.)

When we think about it, this only makes sense. We would never ask a person who does not like children to serve on the children's nurture committee. Likewise, who would invite to join the evangelism committee someone who has no particular convictions regarding Jesus or the church? If the generosity committee's goal is to cast a vision for growing generosity and to accompany fellow travelers along the route to that goal, the only effective guides will be those who are themselves growing in their personal practice of generosity.

Congregations staff their committees in a variety of ways. Mostly, members are assigned, or they are asked to join by a pastor or nominating committee, or in many cases, the congregation invites members to volunteer at will. No matter the process for staffing it, every generosity committee should include only people who believe in and practice generosity. In every staffing model excepting a purely volunteer process, the congregation's treasurer will be asked to verify not the amounts given, but that each potential generosity committee member has a "history of intentional, disciplined, and sacrificial giving to the church." The metric for participation is proportionate giving, not the total given, and in most congregations the treasurer will be the best source for such information. This information will be subjective, as treasurers will find room to define "intentional, disciplined, and sacrificial" in different ways. That said, passing possible generosity committee members through this sifter is far better than filling a committee with members who, in their heart of hearts, either do not believe in the power of generosity or who have not experienced it. The surest way to quell a generosity revolution is to staff the committee who leads it with grumpy or compromised givers.

Should we use a system of pledges? Pledging is the age-old practice of signing a promissory note of sorts, an act of commitment and intention, to share a certain amount of money over a specific time period. Pledges carry an implied moral commitment but not a legal one, and as such, are not binding in any technical or legal sense. While many congregations continue to use a pledge system for both their annual campaign and any capital campaigns, other congregations have experimented with other systems.

Some congregations continue to invite written commitments but have softened the language, abandoning the word pledge for euphemisms like "faith commitment" or "intention of giving." The revised language is meant to comfort the giver, to assure the giver that the promised total amount may be amended, and that the card is not intended to be legally binding. For congregations whose members have unpredictable incomes—farmers, for instance, or people whose incomes depend primarily upon a volatile stock market, or sales commissions—"intention of giving" acknowledges the member's unpredictable financial resources.

Other congregations have altogether abandoned the use of pledge cards, surely evidence of today's rampant and creeping anti-institutionalism. They have replaced pledge cards with multiple, specific appeals, creating a cafeteria model—multiple and frequent requests to fund specific areas of ministry. Such models give members a sense of control about where specifically their money will be used. This sidesteps doubts that the congregation's leadership might use their money in ways they do not approve.

Such systems may avoid the institutional feel of pledge cards and budgets, but they create other challenges as well. Members often tire of seemingly incessant appeals and begin to wonder if they're being nickel-and-dimed to death. Leaders in such congregations often scurry to fund ministries that are less popular.

Most people will fund a housing project before the congregation's office expenses, for instance, but congregations will still have office expenses. Historically, from the institution's perspective, there have been two maxims about funding a budget. First, the institution never receives money it does not ask for, and second, an institution never receives more money than it asks for. The cafeteria-style giving model may ironically prepare members to share less than the model of pledging a percentage of income toward a unified mission and ministry budget.

These are among the reasons I remain partial to the traditional pledge card system for inspiring generosity. There are many motives for retaining the use of pledge cards, and many of the best reasons are not traditional ones. For those older generations likelier to make strong commitments to institutions and to trust them, pledge cards serve the unabashed rationale of helping the congregation's leadership plan for the coming year. For those who love their church and trust its leaders, it is an easy pitch to speak about planning the budget and to use now out-of-vogue words like duty and sacrifice.

Few people think in these terms now. Pledge cards, then—especially if perceived as an institutional instrument intended first to benefit the congregation—are anathema. For those whose life experiences have conditioned them to cynicism about institutions, signing a pledge card is akin to signing a tax form, only without the force of law.

And yet, pledge cards can be dusted off and reinterpreted even to people who view them suspiciously. How? A pledge card is not best intended to benefit the congregation. Certainly, pledge cards are helpful for institutional budgeting and planning. Nonetheless, there are countless congregations who somehow manage to budget without them. And, for people unconvinced about the value of religious institutions, helping a congregation to budget is hardly a motivation to sign a pledge card anyway.

Pledge cards can serve a far higher purpose. Pledge cards can be powerful and intensely personal commitments to personal spiritual development and maturation. A pledge card symbolizes a person's—or an entire household's—promise to be generous with God. It is a token of hope, a talisman of intention, that lifts before the disciple a specific plan for personal spiritual evolution.

In the secular world, pledges are legally binding and purely transactional. They are about exchange, about giving in return for receiving. When we sign a mortgage or a car loan, our signatures embody our word that come what may, we will return the borrowed money. A similar dynamic is true with every floating bill to which we commit, for electricity, for natural gas, for internet connection and cable television and cell phone service.

Early in my adulthood I applied for a car loan. To assess my credit worthiness, the bank's application form called for a list of my monthly payments. The first thing I listed was the family's pledge to the church. "Mr. Travis," the bank officer began, "we are delighted that you give to your church, but at the bank we do not consider your church pledge a debt."

I responded the only way I knew how, which was to explain what I had been taught and the habit I was trying to form. "I understand," I said, "but in my case, if you are evaluating my credit worthiness, you need to know that I do consider it a debt. If push comes to shove, I will pay the church before I pay you." I got the loan. Then, some weeks later, that bank officer joined the congregation I was serving.

I was not threatening the bank with nonpayment. Rather, I was promising myself that the spiritual growth to which I was committing, the spiritual growth possible only with and through intentional, disciplined generosity, could be obtained only by keeping my word to myself. And keeping my word to God. And keeping my word to the congregation. But frankly, keeping my word to the congregation was, for me, third in line.

Pledge cards are the only promissory notes I know of that are purely voluntary, that are not legally binding nor transactional, and yet carry within themselves possibilities for personal transformation. Making a car payment has never, not once, changed my heart. Writing a mortgage check has never, not once, lifted my gaze to God. Paying an electricity bill, a gas bill, an internet bill, has never, not once, redirected my soul to eternal principles or set my spirit ablaze with the wild-eyed notion that I have it within me to become a better human being. Signing a pledge card has done, at least for me, every one of these things.

Another advantage of pledge cards and pledge systems is that they encourage not one-time giving, not singular impulsive acts of kindness, but regular, systematic, and long-term generosities. Hilary Davidson and Christian Smith have published the findings of a systematic study of generosity in the United States. Not only do they conclude that generosity leads to personal happiness—they have the studies to prove it. There is more. Committed, intentional, disciplined generosity can be distinguished from happenchance, one gift at a time generosity. "Our emphasis here," they say, "is on *practices* of generosity, not on single generous acts. What matters about practices, compared to one-time acts, is that they are *repeated behaviors that involve recurrent intention and attention*"[3] (italics mine).

Pledging inspires regular giving, consistent generosity. As I mentioned on pages 22–23, a member of a congregation I once served offered an incredible illustration about the beauty of regular generosity. Retired, he received a singular Social Security check each month, and his bank charged a fee for each check he wrote. To avoid unnecessary bank fees, he offered his pledge to the congregation with one check a month, but this left a problem. So, on the intervening Sundays, he simply dropped an empty offering envelope into the passing plate because, he said, he never wanted a child to see the offering plate pass him without him placing something into it.

A pledge card is easily reinterpreted even to the skeptical, even to the cynical, as an object of personal devotion capable of vaporizing our resistance and enlivening our souls. By promising ourselves, our families, and our God that we will share, off the top of our incomes, on a regular basis, in an intentional way, holds us accountable to our aspirations in some way like committing to a regular exercise program does, or to a weight reduction diet. But pledging is far more transformational than run-of-the-mill New Year's resolutions. Pledging taps our truthfulness. Pledging inspires our integrity. Pledging plays its part in our ongoing redemption as children of God.

Should the pastor share how much she gives? A jaundiced America now looks suspiciously at even the concept of leadership. Conditioned to disappointment, we are hardly surprised any longer by our leaders' failures and hypocrisies. Leadership has earned a black eye and a dirty name in this anti-institutional age. How regularly do you read or watch or hear another story of a leader whose carefully crafted public persona is shown to be a ruse, a social media construction?

This is true of government officials, educators, and business leaders, so it's no surprise that such instincts have made their way into the church. The default cynicism doubts that leaders have their followers' best interests at heart and wonders if leaders authentically practice the life they give the appearance of leading. Pastors are by and large genuine people, and few seem consumed with curating a public persona. The challenge is that we swim in the cultural stew with charlatans who do.

When it comes to giving money, this is a dynamic we must understand, deserved or not. Some church members believe that their pastors give no personal money to the church at all.

To younger church members, or to those altogether new to the faith, it can seem a strange calculus that the pastor is paid by the congregation to which he then returns a portion of his earnings. I made sure every Sunday morning that the ushers offered me a chance to add my envelope to the offering plate just to assure that people understood my passion to share in the church's mission.

If some members are surprised to learn that their pastors give anything to the church, others will be surprised to learn how much. The skeptical parishioner might agree that a pastor contributes a small amount to keep up appearances, or perhaps from a sense of duty, but imagine their thoughts upon learning that the pastor is in fact attempting to lead the life she's recommending for others. The natural reaction of a reluctant parishioner upon hearing that the pastor has pledged ten percent of her salary toward the church's ministry might be greater than mere surprise. Likely, it's a jaw-dropping, thought-provoking discovery. "Well, I'll be," you can imagine him thinking, "she actually means it. She truly tithes her income."

Should the pastor share with the congregation's leadership how much she gives? Absolutely. Without a doubt. Even politicians share this information, releasing their tax forms—complete with charitable giving—both when running for and when holding public office. In this cynical age, transparency is the surest and fastest route toward building trust in leadership.

Whether the pastor shares this information with congregational leaders in a meeting, or with the congregation from the pulpit, or both, is the pastor's choice. Should the pastor share this info only with the board, the information will quickly reach the rest of the congregation anyway. You can bank on it.

Should the pastor share that "I tithe," or should he make public the actual dollar amount he pledges? The congregation knows what the pastor is paid, of course, so given the complexity of a pastor's terms of call—with housing allowances, social security offsets, and other compensations and reimbursements—simply announcing that you tithe will raise more questions than it answers. Tithe on what? Pre-tax or post-tax? Housing allowance and salary, or only salary? We'll think in greater depth about the tithe in the next chapter, but for the moment note my confidence that sharing the actual dollar amount is necessary transparency. It will shine light towards the cynic's final corner, where she sheepishly hopes to find some evidence that the authority figure isn't honestly practicing the generosity she preaches.

You might think that explaining yourself to cynics is a sorry reason to reveal such personal information, and you would be right if this was the only justification for such candor. It isn't. The far better reason for sharing the amount pledged is the magnificent trust it engenders between pastor and people. Upon hearing the pastor's commitment in dollars, some find themselves inspired, possessed of the new thought that if the pastor can share sacrificially, so can they. Others find themselves awakened, realizing that they make well in excess of the pastor's salary and have yet shared less. Others, surprised by the confidence such a decision requires, are drawn into a new circle of trust; they begin to see that truly, the church can be an authentic experience of community different from any others to which they belong. Such truth-telling serves also to build a congregation's trust in its pastor or pastors. It says, "I am here with you, genuinely committed to our shared ministries."

Nothing builds trust in leadership so thoroughly as, well, leadership.

Still, Jesus is in our hearts and heads. "But when you give alms, do not let your left hand know what your right hand is doing, so that your alms may be done in secret; and your Father who sees in secret will reward you" (Matt. 6:3–4). Can pastors share information as personal as giving intentions without directly violating—in spirit if not by technicality—what appears to be a clear biblical imperative?

Matthew 6 isolates the tripod of ancient Jewish piety—almsgiving, praying, and fasting—and instructs that each are to be practiced either "in secret," or before our "Father who is in secret." Clearly, the church has never taken this text so literally that it has forbidden public prayers, or failed to recommend fasting, or been wholly private about almsgiving. You need look no farther than Ananias and Sapphira, or to Lydia of Thyatira, to know that the early church shared such information (Acts 5:1–11, 16:11–15).

What can Matthew's sixth chapter mean to us? Motivation is the heart of the matter—engaging spiritual practices with a pure heart, doing the right things and for the right reasons. Jesus wants us on guard against our self-promoting instincts, hopes our religious practices will be driven by our desire to glorify God, not to glorify ourselves. Strictly speaking, then, it isn't good enough to do the right thing for the wrong reasons, yet Freud was hardly the first to notice that none of us does anything for singular reasons. Human beings are a complex mix of motivations, pure and impure, holy and profane, conscious and hidden, clear and cloudy. Our highest spiritual aspiration is always the honest pursuit of holy motivations, and because purely virtuous motives are always aspirational, and because Homo sapiens are what we are, we will often fall short. This is the nature of all religious practice.

Pastors are reluctant to share our giving patterns generally because two unholy motivations troll our souls; either we fear showboating, lording our financial faithfulness for the adulation of others, or we fear embarrassment, that people will think we could be giving more. Fair enough.

Yet, if we are to take the central theological point of Matthew 6 seriously—that our hope in religious practices is to glorify God—transparent pastors can choose to share our giving details from an authentic desire to share what we have learned; namely, at least in my life, that God has showered me with abundance, that I respond sacrificially to be in synchronicity with the Giver, and that as I do so I know God more deeply and myself more fully. Bluntly, given the splendor and power of these affirmations, it would be malpractice not to share my giving intentions.

So in the end, a pastor's decision to share how much she gives engages the precise struggle as choosing to become more generous in the first place; in your heart of hearts, do you trust God's provision? If you long to trust your parishioners, have you given them warrant to trust you? What seems at first a practical question is even more fundamentally a spiritual one. The pastor's inner dialogue writes the subsequent conversation to be had with church leaders.

Pastors who wrestle with these questions and then opt for transparency will be amazed at the ripples of grace echoing through their congregations. When you see how your generosity experience will help those you also lead, false motives will fall away. As it always does, this decision depends upon your inner life.

Should the pastor know how much others give? Here is the most sensitive question of all. Here, time and again, I have watched pastors draw their lines in this sand. The words spoken in such conversations are genuinely civil, but opinions—and biases—run deep.

For pastors who steadfastly refuse to look at congregational giving records, the litany of objections is short. They fear that it will shape their opinions of individual church members. They fear judgment—not only that church members will judge them, but that they will come to judge individual church members. They fear the temptation to think about and to treat church members differently based upon their giving histories, kowtowing to big givers while neglecting small givers. They fear, too, that church members will assume that they prefer wealthier, more generous givers, and that these perceptions will diminish their leadership to the whole congregation. They fear that they will be unable to keep such information confidential. They fear, in other words, the implicit power (and hence responsibility) that such information presents.

These are important fears. I daresay that there isn't a pastor alive whose imagination doesn't paint an instant image when asked to name a financially self-interested pastor who leads a church with ulterior fiscal motives. Can you see him? He is a backslapping, ingratiating, silver-tongued devil, the megachurch pastor in search of the megadonor. She kowtows to wealthy people, granting them pardon no matter how they have come by their wealth, always genuflecting so long as their money keeps coming. He visits wealthy church members in hospitals and in homes, but he is rarely seen in the company of the congregation's less wealthy. He grovels and fawns. She is obsequious, sycophantic.

Who wants to be *that* pastor?

Growing up a West Texas Presbyterian taught me a great deal about implicit bias. Implicit bias is an association, belief, or feeling about some other group of people. Always unconscious, such bias correlates certain qualities and behaviors with whole groups, never mind that no quality or characteristic ever marks every member of a group no matter how homogenous. Never mind also that the utter injustice of assuming that simply because a person belongs within some larger group, he must necessarily exhibit stereotypes about it.

West Texas Presbyterians go to great lengths to behave in certain ways lest someone think we are Southern Baptists. We dance in public, tell bawdy jokes, use carefully planned bad language, and relish being seen in liquor stores, all to avoid association with the perceived false piety and self-claimed biblical literalism we unconsciously assume to be universally shared by all Southern Baptists. Evil rests, we are fond of saying, not in the thing itself, but in the abuse of it. All things in moderation.

This is implicit bias. I have spent a lifetime unpeeling the subtle conditioning of my childhood and confronting myself over this unjust bias, but still I am certain that my intolerance will be pointed out as I cross the judgment seat.

A good many pastors have a similar bias toward pastors who review congregational giving records. For some pastors, a pastor reviewing records—giving histories or giving intentions—draws to mind *that* pastor.

It shouldn't.

Pastors should regularly review their congregation's giving records. Doing so hardly makes one an ecclesial charlatan. In reality, knowing how much members give can be an integral part of humble, effective generosity leadership.

Let's call a pastor's review of giving records "generosity knowledge." Likewise, let's label a pastor's choice not to review such records "generosity ignorance."

Generosity knowledge is a key pastoral tool because, unsurprisingly, generosity is often an indicator of either spiritual health or of spiritual threat. For instance, if a member or member family has a history of disciplined generosity with the congregation, and their giving nonetheless increases substantially, imagine the conversation to be had when the pastor phones to say thank you. What led to the increase? Is there a spiritual dynamic to the surge? How can the pastor and congregation support this stretch, and what lessons can be learned from these now even more passionate givers?

Likewise, a sudden drop in giving is always a tipoff that a giver needs pastoral attention. Most frequently, dips in giving indicate a change in employment or economic status or that the congregant has grown disenchanted with the church. When making the pastoral follow-up, the pastor doesn't necessarily ask about giving at all. Rather, she asks, "How are you?

What's going on in your life?" If the parishioner faces financial hardship, this conversation is the place to celebrate that the congregation doesn't want the member's money so much as the congregation wants the member, as a human being, as a disciple. I've lost count of members who, being reminded of this, took a relieved breath, let go of their needless guilt, and continued active ministry in the church.

Since independent and individualistic Americans are conditioned to send messages with our money, it behooves the church to learn the language of those who think of money in these ways. So, "How are you?" will reveal such challenges as troubled marriages, chemical addictions, and often anger with the congregation. With the problem named, the pastor and parishioner may work together to address the dilemma.

(On a related note, I find fascinating that church members would willingly share with me their most painful dilemmas—affairs, abortions, addictions, mental health challenges, broken relationships, existential crises—yet some would cordon off financial giving as too personal to share with a pastor. Paradoxically, such members take in stride the reality that another staff person, or volunteer, will indeed know their giving amounts. Surely such thinking doesn't appraise the pastor less trustworthy than these others. Is this bifurcation in thinking built upon our society's sacralization of money?)

Some pastors want to avoid even the impression that they treat large givers differently than smaller givers, but generosity ignorance can't shield the pastor from such perceptions. If a parishioner is already so cynical, so jaundiced, that he thinks his pastor guilty of favoring the wealthy, a broadly shared knowledge that the pastor doesn't look at giving amounts will not convince the critic of anything. In fact, a church member already so jaundiced would have to conclude only that the ingratiating pastor was showing favoritism based only on guesswork, hardly a credential in the cynic's way of thinking.

If a pastor suffers an inner temptation to cater to the wealthy, generosity ignorance won't protect the pastor. After all, a pastor hardly need review giving records to be a flunky for the wealthy. Our culture is quite adept at signaling wealth. The clothes we wear, the homes we inhabit, the cars we drive, the diplomas we hang, all of it provides an abundance of information about our financial capabilities. Like everyone else in a church, over time the pastor deduces who has wealth, who wants wealth, and who is uninterested in wealth. If in her heart a pastor wants to please the wealthy, generosity knowledge is hardly necessary. As with all such challenges, the solution must come from the pastor's inner life.

Generosity knowledge invites pastors to connect givers with the ministries they care most about, and this enriches the congregation's ministries over time. Armed with such knowledge, the pastor may invite greater giving from the giver while also using the gift to relieve pressure in other areas of the congregation's budget. The pastor also knows to keep that member informed on any progress in the giver's beloved ministry, which both deepens the giver's joy and expands the ministry.

Generosity knowledge also allows the pastor to counter any systematic, behind-the-scenes manipulation sometimes perpetuated by ungenerous people who nonetheless give the studied impression that they are big givers. Churches include human beings, which is to say that church members are hardly untouched by an instinct for self-advancement and control, and one method to practice both is to give false impressions about one's generosity. It often works, too—unless an authority figure in the system knows the truth and counters the manipulation. Pastors are best placed to play this role.

Generosity knowledge also guides the pastor in preparing the congregation for the future. The financial health, even the viability, of many mainline congregations is now in peril, and it has changed drastically in the last three decades. When I entered ministry in the early 1990s, the rule of thumb was that 20 percent of a church's membership contributed 80 percent of the average congregation's budget. Church stewardship professionals are now saying that this reality has grown even more lopsided, with many congregations facing a 10/90 percent variance. Add to this disproportion that almost always the small group of big givers is aged, and you can easily see the peril of generosity ignorance. Some congregations are quite simply a death, disagreement, or transfer away from insolvency, and if the pastor doesn't look at giving records, the only people who know it are the large contributors and a paid or volunteer treasurer. Armed with this knowledge, a pastor can work with the giver to prepare for what is coming, perhaps through an end-of-life gift to endow the giver's contributions, or perhaps a gradual tapering off to allow the congregation to enlarge the financial base.

Generosity knowledge sensitizes the pastor to a greater breadth of spiritual depth. There is a presumption in some of Christianity that all wealth is intrinsically denigrating, that wealth is incompatible with Christian discipleship. Given our biblical conviction that God exercises an option for the poor, some reason conversely that God either condemns, or at best neglects, the wealthy. Earlier chapters in this book deal head on with the ethical and spiritual dilemmas posed by wealth accumulation, consumerism, and acquisitiveness, yet my pastoral experience has shown me that many of the church's healthiest and most spiritually mature members are also persons of wealth. Having wrestled with wealth's temptations, they possess a hard-earned wisdom about wealth's possibilities, also. Spiritually, wealth is blessing or curse. Its owner must decide.

Conversely, many of our poorest parishioners face enormous spiritual challenge. God may indeed exercise an option for the poor, but such divine attention is interested in more than evening the scales. It also cares about the spiritual health of those who are poor because poverty brings its own share of spiritual confrontations: resentment, anger, jealousy, and a diminished sense of self and one's possibilities in the world. Many Christians have an implicit bias, carried within the faith construct, that because God raises the lowly and humbles the wealthy, that wealth is wholly evil and poverty somehow irreversibly noble. It turns out that life is more complex than this. Money cannot buy happiness, but the lack of it can make a firm down payment on spiritual turmoil.

In the end, pastors of good conscience will decide differently on reviewing financial giving records. I remain convinced, however, and observe to you, that transformational generosity ministry requires the pastor to cultivate generosity knowledge.

On tithing

Should we teach the tithe? The first section of this book wrestled with the question, "Why should I be generous?" The biblical tithe begs the question, "Why should I be generous with the church?"

The biblical tithe is withered and worn. Most Christians have been at least exposed to the idea of the tithe—the biblical teaching to give 10 percent of our income—and many were taught as children that tithing is mandatory. Some have misused the tithe as a biblical bludgeoning tool, a guilt-inducing battering ram of legalistic bossiness. Others have dismissed the tithe as Old Testament detritus, swept away with other juridical expectations since Jesus's followers have been freed from the letter of the law. Still others would dismiss the tithe as outdated and anachronistic, yet Jesus praises the widow whose meager mite continues to ring true across these many centuries.

The truth lies somewhere in between.

I have never been much interested in obtuse arguments about the tithe being normative for Christians. There are those who do treat the tithe as a tax, while the tithe is better seen, unexpectedly enough, as a tip—that which we happily share as a grateful response. Most mainline pastors have great reticence about mechanistically drawing mandatory pronouncements from Scripture because doing so with ethical maxims you think divinely required leaves you intellectually bound to defend those you do not, or at least to explain the inconsistency. Can some biblical maxims be duty while others are contextualized and laid aside? Is the biblical prohibition against killing equal to its commandments not to eat shrimp or wear tattoos? The answer is not to set aside all biblical commandments but rather to interpret them outside of a deontological framework.

So, has the tithe been repealed? The apostle Paul, when dealing with the law's requirements, suggests that our measure should not be legality but rather utility. "'All things are lawful for me,' but not all things are beneficial" (1 Cor. 6:12a). As a pastor, and therefore as a practical theologian, this concept is useful both as a teaching tool and also as a biblical interpretation strategy. The question is not, then, "Is a practice required?" but rather, "Is a practice beneficial?" Beneficial to whom, and for what reason? Add this to the question, "Did Jesus have anything to say on the matter?" and we find a framework for our thinking.

I am convinced that sharing at least 10 percent of one's financial resources is practically, and spiritually, beneficial. It is helpful personally, for it plants trust in God and in God's provision, and it ushers us into practicing generosity with God. Tithing is helpful communally, for it provides resources for Christ's church to engage in mission and ministry, within and beyond its walls. Tithing is helpful socially, for it provides Christian witness as the church partners with the Holy Spirit in God's ongoing redemption and restoration of the world. Tithing is a time-tested and age-old spiritual discipline which, to my mind, is disregarded only by obtuse rationalization. Not everyone can tithe, but everyone can aspire to tithe.

The tithe—appropriately framed and interpreted—has yet another benefit. Traditional nomenclature had it that when we share of our resources, we return *"God's* tithe and our offerings."* While many modern congregations have slipped into returning *"our* tithes and offerings," the older language rings the more basic truth, that everything we have fundamentally belongs to God. Giving *our* tithes is the exact opposite of returning *God's* tithe; one focuses on us and what we do, while the other dwells upon God and what God has already done.

There is something both challenging yet comforting in remembering that we own nothing. After all, human beings are renters, here but for a short while. We leave the world as naked as we enter it. As the Irish have it, you will find no pocket in a shroud. As I approach my own death, "returning God's tithe" has a liberating resonance. "Returning God's tithe" is a down-canyon echo of "returning to God." It reminds us to invest in eternal things that last and not in those that rot and rust. The very concept of "God's tithe" shapes our priorities and molds our values.

It is helpful to remember that a full 10 percent tithe is a new goal for most people, and audacious at that. Even for those convinced of the beauty of proportionate giving, leaping from 1 or 2 percent to ten, all at once, might be overwhelming. For many, then, a 10 percent tithe is aspirational, part of generosity's long-range plan. Particularly with young adults, just beginning their professional lives, a 10 percent tithe might appear so out of reason as to be damaging. This is why they must begin at the beginning, where they are, at 1 or 2 percent.

Some suggest, because many people are simply unable to spare 10 percent, that presenting its possibility is irretrievably unpastoral. This is akin to a doctor neglecting to recommend exercise because at present the patient's ankle is sprained. While it's true that a twisted ankle rules out a marathon, there is much the patient can do to be healthier until the current constraint is removed. In the meantime, a limited exercise regimen is life-giving and helps the patient both to be healthy in the moment and to prepare for a future when marathons are a possibility. I learned early in ministry never to underestimate the work of the Holy Spirit by challenging people with lesser aspirations. Neglecting to teach the tithe out of pastoral concerns, though well-intentioned, is nonetheless ultimately patronizing, even arrogant.

People wonder, is 10 percent figured on my gross income or my net income? Sometimes, when I am asked about figuring the tithe on gross versus net income, I suggest working toward a tithe on net income and then reevaluating. "See how it feels," I say, "then decide whether you will stretch out toward a tithe on your gross income." Other times, if I know the person well, I say, "Use the income you report to the bank, not the Internal Revenue Service." Frankness has its place. I know almost no one who, having set and reached a goal of giving 10 percent of their net income, has not moved on to tithe upon their gross income. Likewise, I know of many who, having reached a tithe upon their gross income, have continued to give yet more.

Is a tithe the goal or the starting point? If the tithe is to be beneficial, it can be neither a coercive nor a constraining legalism. A joyous giver does not regard a tithe as obligatory or as a limitation. Rather, it invites us into relationship, a friendship within which our partner helps us to explore gratitude, what we legitimately need, and how we share with others who have legitimate need.

Does the tithe include more than money? Indeed. A full-bodied teaching of the biblical tithe includes much more than mere money. As "the earth is the LORD's and all that is in it" (Ps. 24:1), returning to God that which already belongs to God is a liberating and exciting thought. What creativity is released when we imagine returning to God some healthy portion of our energy and our attention, our interests and our instincts, the clothes in our closets and the furniture stored in our garages, not to mention our time. Frederick Buechner made the interesting point that Lent—the 40 days plus Sundays preceding Easter—is essentially a tithe of the year. Any Lenten discipline is therefore a tithe of time.[4] Tithing includes our money, and, thanks be to God, so much more.

The church defaults to monetary thinking when it comes to tithing. It's easily measured, after all, and therefore simpler to calculate than the often-remarkable time that members give the church. Particularly for younger families, who often have more time than money, celebrating non-monetary contributions is not only pastoral—it is honest.

Sometimes, people with financial means hoard their money while rationalizing that they have given otherwise of their time and talent. The opposite practice—giving money while withholding time and talent—is also common. One study revealed a surprising pattern, that the greater the financial gift to the congregation, the more infrequent the worship and participation in the community. The author entitled his paper "Pay or Pray."[5] While this is unusual—typically frequent worship attendance leads to higher giving—this study reveals a different and equally mischievous quid pro quo with God. In this thinking, giving money substitutes for giving time and talent, or in other words, giving of oneself.

Some people tithe their incomes in order not to engage in worship or mission. Entire congregations sometimes do a similar thing. How many congregations are willing to write checks for favored mission projects but will not dare engage the recipients of their generosity face-to-face? Writing checks and authorizing Visa withdrawals is often far easier than the bother of participating in the life of the church, and simpler than meeting the guests at a food pantry or homeless shelter. A hope implicit in most mission is that those who have means will meet and enter relationship with those who do not. The missional impulse bends toward relationship, not only justice and/or mercy.

Again, a full-bodied teaching of the biblical tithe includes much more than mere money. The central tenets of tithing—proportionate giving, and God's ownership of all that we have—can be remarkably and redemptively inspirational as we grow in generosity.

People wonder, does all of God's tithe go to my local church or might I share some of it with other worthy organizations?

The philanthropic landscape has changed irreversibly over the last fifty years, particularly as denominational centralism has waned. Many denominational ministries are now funded outside of traditional denominational funding streams—to which congregations contribute— and must now fend for themselves. Colleges and universities, seminaries, children's homes, camp and conference centers, and so on, formerly buttressed by denominational coffers, must now replace the funding that once flowed from centralized funding. Surely sharing a portion of God's tithes with such bona fide church ministries is in keeping with the intention and spirit of the tithe itself.

Add to the list of ministries formerly funded from denominational treasuries the catalogue of not-for-profit organizations, which has exploded in recent decades. American Christians are besieged with charitable requests. Colleges and universities, hospitals and disease-specific research efforts, environmental and anti-poverty groups, international disaster relief and economic aid organizations combine into a powerful and compelling solicitation machine. Next consider that many of these organizations do the very things the church is called to do, or that the church used to do. And, remember that many of these organizations do these things efficiently and well.

Decades ago, for instance, most mainline denominations had national offices addressing homelessness. Today, congregations of those same mainline denominations have overwhelmingly chosen to support independent Habitat for Humanity, so these denominationally directed mainline efforts have withered away.

Homelessness is hardly the only example of parachurch and nonprofit organizations doing what has been the church's historic work, and nobly so, ably so. Think about the hospitals and schools in your community. Consider the literacy programs and the clothing closets, the soup kitchens and the food pantries, the homeless shelters, the adoption agencies and the counseling ministries. Consider the United Way, a community agency raising dollars destined for a variety of organizations addressing an assortment of carefully targeted local needs.

Surely, we wonder, these organizations deserve a portion of God's tithe. Certainly they are doing God's work. Should not our tithing include them?

Faithful people will reach differing decisions on this question. The Christian faithfulness of an organization's mission may well have nothing to do with its denominational affiliation or particular theological identity. Indeed, evaluated by standard efficiency measures, some organizations conduct mission more resourcefully than the church does. (This, by the way, is a call to every congregation to study its philanthropic competition for lessons about using God's dollars as effectively and efficiently as not-for-profits must prove that they do.)

Since reasonable people will come to different conclusions on this question, I offer quietly my own answer. As for me and my house, we will give 10 percent of our income to our local congregation. (In Presbyterian polity, this means that we also contribute to a bevy of denominational ministries—across the nation and globe—as our congregation contributes to the denomination's broader efforts.) Beyond the tithe, we will give more modest amounts to our favorite charities and causes.

My family's answer is genuine, though I recognize that tithing a full 10 percent to our congregation carries an implicit tension. In this anti-institutional era, Christians seek trustworthy congregations. One significant measure of trustworthiness is a congregation's primary focus: is it wholly invested in the spiritual growth and maturity of its membership? Is it passionately committed to following Jesus wherever he may lead, or is it more concerned with its own institutional survival and well-being? If the church is more interested in the spiritual strength of its members than in its institutional perpetuation, if the church preaches that our individual and familial need to give is more important than the church's need to receive, then it would be wholly disingenuous for that church also to say, in effect, that I need to give, and that I need to give first and only to the local church. If intentional and disciplined generosity is good for our souls, surely the church must leave to its members all decisions as to where we share God's money. The paradox is obvious.

So, I freely choose to return God's tithe to my local congregation. A congregation that genuinely teaches and models the joys of generosity, and also invites me into the freedom of choice, wins my trust and my tithe. (Of course, this assumes that the congregation is also engaged in transformational ministry, in worship, education, and mission.)

I realize that this practice is rare and becoming more so. Others are choosing differently. I understand why. Yet in the end, our baptisms and our deaths are parenthetical reference points for all that comes between. For those who crave to follow Jesus, for people who long to build their lives upon God's love and dreams, and who blossom when living in community with those who crave the same, for these people both the front and the back doors are hinged in the local church. We cannot live fully Christian lives in isolation. People rarely grow in generosity in isolation from others who are seeking to do the same. The local parish is God's response.

I rejoice that tithing has not been repealed. Our teaching on tithing, appropriately interpreted and practiced, remains a healthy, helpful, and time-tested guide and goal. Healthy congregations can teach and interpret the tithing principle with neither doctrinal rigidity nor biblical embarrassment.

CONCLUSION

Is the Church Theologically Unique?

I CONCLUDE WHERE I BEGAN, WRITING FROM A HOSPICE BED, GAZ-ing mindfully through the opposite wall, marveling at the embarrassment of riches that has been my life. I am cocooned in gratitude, wide-eyed to God's countless gifts, cascading even now in these waning months.

Some believe that, in the exact instant we die, our entire lives flash before our eyes. Some even speculate that such a review is our personal sins highlight reel, preparing us for the judgment seat. But what if God grants a last millisecond, mind's eye journey through our lives not as an exit evaluation, but rather as a reminder of God's gifts? What if, just as the last remnants of oxygen wander from our brains, God parts the curtains of consciousness for a movie premiere featuring those glorious moments when God met our needs, answered our prayers, and showered us in purpose and in joy? This is the speculation I prefer! It keeps me gazing at the wall, wondering what I will see when my time comes.

Most of my highlight reel will have been shot at church. This surprises me because, well, I have mixed feelings about the institutional church.

On first thought, having grown up in the church, as one of four generations of preachers, and having at least tried to serve faithfully the institutional church for thirty years, I confess that I love the church. Upon deeper thought, I suspect that the institutional church sometimes makes "Jesus want to drink gin straight out of the cat dish."[1] How could it be otherwise? The church aspires to model divinity, so its failures are glaringly obvious and all-the-more heartbreaking.

I can see them now, the ordinary moments, expected and otherwise, when God's finger touched my being through the institutional church, the baptisms, the weddings, the funerals. I remember the summer camps, the Sunday evening youth group meetings, the vacation church school Bible lessons. I remember the mission trips, the session meetings, the presbytery gatherings, the national denominational meetings. I recall the countless conversations, the sermon discussions, the long days at the office, the counseling sessions. So many of these memories were and are life-giving, beautiful, holy even. Through the church, God called, challenged, nourished, and molded me. Truth be told, most everything I am and believe, I owe to the church.

There is a difference between the institutional church and the intense, passionate community I experience in the local congregation. For lack of better nomenclature, let's speak of the church-as-organization and the church-as-community. They are intertwined within a symbiotic relationship, making any ultimate distinction between them impossible, feeding one another as they do, pressed up against the other.

The church-as-organization includes the church at all its levels—international, denominational, national, regional, and local (at least insofar as the local congregation relates to the broader church). The church-as-organization concerns itself with order and ecumenical relationships, with doctrine and structure, with policies and standards. The church-as-organization approves meeting minutes, favors parliamentary procedure, and uses a great deal of paper. It seeks to build relationships between institutions even while constructing the very doctrinal and polity particularities that make those relationships complex to build.

The church-as-community is fascinated most fundamentally with relationships, relationships with God and with one another. It is consumed with the values of the kingdom of heaven, including love, justice, gratitude, forgiveness, inclusion, joy, humility, equality, and shared bounty. Its tools include Scripture, the sacraments, worship, prayer, and truth-telling. God may not be conjured, but God may certainly be invited, so the church-as-community fosters shared experiences of divine love. The church-as-community is holy antidote to our chief fear—isolation—and holy cure for our primary illness—guilt.

I love the church-as-community. I understand the church-as-organization. When I speak of the institutional church, I mean to include both, in some ways an inseparable amalgam. When I speak of the church-as-community only, I am quite capable of sentimentalizing it.

That's a problem. Because the church-as-organization is also exhibit A for jaded hypocrisy, contorted priorities, and broken hopes.

My mixed feelings are no different from yours, though I certainly bring a multigenerational, insider perspective. Alongside all the transformational recollections of church in my highlight reel, will I see, too, snapshots of pettiness and disappointment—my own and others? Will I see again how the church excuses so many wrongs? I remember the church's complicity in wars, its comfort with racism, its searing teachings on human sexuality, and its functional misogyny. Maddeningly,

I recognize that the church-as-organization has largely sold out to creeping materialism, bought in to consumerism, and offered at best a fainthearted rival to unregulated capitalism even amidst the greatest wealth disparity in our nation's history. And if this weren't enough, we have offered a faith easily compromised by uncritical patriotism and a bureaucracy awash in embarrassingly human machinations.

If the American church goes the way of European Christianity, it will not be because conventional Christians have lost their trust in Jesus Christ. It will be because everyday Christians lose their conviction that the church is capable of visualizing and leading such transformational change, or more basically perhaps, that American Christians have lost the hope that such transformational change is even possible.

Pastors, imagine yourself at a retreat center with other pastors. After a full day of goings-on, your mind is spinning, your heart is open, and finally you settle into a booth at a local pub. It is a trusted atmosphere and you feel vulnerable, yet strangely comfortable being so. Another pastor redirects the conversation with something she has been wondering. She asks, "Do we still believe that the church can show the way into God's promised future? Do we still believe that wars will cease, that peace and justice can prevail, that all peoples shall come streaming to God, and that the creation may yet be saved from environmental disaster? Do we remain convinced that the church is Christ's body, and that God gives regular glimpses of this coming reality and charges it with modeling God's reign for the world to see and trust?"

She continues, "What are you doing to build your parish into a generosity church, with love and grace, gratitude and generosity?"

In the last chapter, we considered the impulse to support other worthy organizations because they do the things the church does, or used to do, or should do. That impulse exposes a reductionist and culturally conditioned understanding of the church's identity and mission. Are function and efficiency the criteria upon which we are to understand the church? Is the church to be evaluated and measured based only upon what it *does*? Or, are we also to consider what the church *is*—the body of Christ, called into being and nourished by God's Holy Spirit, the covenantal family into which God calls those whom God baptizes, God's worshiping people nourished at God's table and pulpit, that eclectic and subversive community intended to embody and offer glimpses of the coming kingdom of heaven?

Do you sense as I do that many mainline parishioners have simply lost this vision? Clearly, some have concluded that the church is not theologically distinct, no different than most other human institutions, not really. Oh, our faith in Jesus remains strong, but our frustrations with the church have led many to abandon "organized religion," and many who remain in the church see it functionally only, practically, but not theologically. "Oh, the church still does many good things. It provides community for belonging, and it meets our need for ritual, and it does good things in the community. Like a lot of organizations."

We haven't necessarily made a conscious decision to think this way. It has happened slowly, over time, where it's less likely noticed. There was no bang; it was a long, strained whimper. But it's true; most mainline American Protestants have come to see the church in merely human terms, not ontologically different from most other human institutions, like the Rotary Club, but with a Jesus veneer. We treat the church—in our thinking *and in our giving*—as one more organization in a rather long and growing list of human institutions which do generally good and helpful things. We have downgraded the church. Does it sometimes seem to you, too, that for many, the church is the United Way with a cross on the wall?

These are the places my mind wanders to in this hospice bed.

Just then, I remember my love affair with the church, at least with the church-as-community. I have story after story featuring run-of-the-mill Christians doing impossibly gracious things, redemptive things. In my own life God has offered scenes of holy breakthrough, one after another, in which I have watched, astounded, the Spirit at work.

In a nation possessed of the projected myth of self-made people, I have seen everyday Christians celebrate the beauty and power of interdependence. In a day when public Christianity is irreversibly compromised by its lust for political power, I have witnessed everyday Christians leverage their meager influence in favor of the forgotten and the outcast. In a society besot with ambitions of competition, control, and ultimately oppression, I watched for thirty years of ministry as humble disciples trusted in the contrasting possibilities of vulnerability and cooperation. Convinced as we are that Jesus was scapegoated and that therefore his followers cannot stand idly by as the culture scapegoats additional innocents, I have watched the church defend immigrants and minorities of many sorts. In a time of rampant loneliness and isolation, I have witnessed the church as authentic community, "where sin is forgiven, reconciliation is accomplished, and the dividing walls of hostility are torn down."[2]

In lives of worship, study, fellowship, and service, the church has a way of, well, making Christians. No other institution makes Christians, and one wonders, if the church withers, who will?

When all is said and done, the church has a unique—and therefore irreplaceable—gift for the world. The church remains, despite its flaws and failures, the body of Jesus Christ.

The church at its best invites us to join in and to model values that neither rot nor rust. The church is the only institution to which I remain voluntarily committed to relationships with people I may not even like, and without being paid to, like the workplace. The church is the only institution that taught my children the beauty of giving things away without expectation of exchange or compensation. The church is the only institution to tend my family's most important transitions—births, marriages, illnesses, relocations, and deaths—and also weep with us through the divorces, disappointments, and outright failures.

To Christians who cannot say that their congregation is theologically unique, maybe it isn't. The answer is not to abandon it. The answer is to renew it.

Turns out, on the far side of mixed feelings, I retain great hope for the church. The world needs the church to be the church, right now. A divided, angry nation and a seriously endangered world need desperately to know the redemptive possibilities of sacrificial love and unexpected reconciliation. Untold people, isolated and cynical, fearful and wounded, crave a foretaste of God's coming kingdom of radical inclusion, mutual peace, and unmerited grace.

If you want to understand generosity, search for God. If you want to learn to be more generous, find a healthy and grateful church.

I began the twenty-first century by moving to a new congregation, in January of 2000. The earliest days of that pastorate I spent as pastors always do, getting acquainted, learning who's who, discerning what was sacred for this community. When newly arrived pastors survey the field, we're on the lookout for that core of exceptionally committed members, the families who are or who did raise their kids in the congregation, the leaders whom other members have long respected, the saints and curmudgeons who form the fellowship's nucleus.

In this new call I soon met Bill and Kathi Rito, an ordained elder and ordained deacon, respectively, raising their three boys. They were the sort of parishioners ministers long for: humble, sensible, and generous, and they were present every time the church opened its doors. Theirs was a quiet faith, evident in everything they did. With a cluster of disciples like Kathi and Bill, it's plain fun to serve a congregation. The church's work not only gets done; it radiates purpose, it exudes authenticity. With such people the congregation feels like an ancient olive tree, or maybe an unsinkable ship. Either way, it conveys heft, gravitas, a sense of connection to something timeless, and for a pastor new to a congregation, meeting such people is like meeting an adult sibling separated since birth; though you're only just meeting, you intuit and assume shared commitments, powerful values, and a common vision. Such people make being the latest to arrive much less lonely.

Kathi had come by her faithfulness rightly, growing up in a nearby congregation where both of her parents—Charlie and Marilyn (Lynne) Higgins—were core leaders. They were classic social justice Protestants, called in their faith life to community service outside the congregation. Charlie was an ordained deacon and had been elected to the school board for decades. Lynne had served as elder and Sunday school teacher in the church, and also as a Girl Scout leader and city councilwoman. In fact, Lynne had grown into a noted public servant, sitting on the local housing commission, as the governor's appointee to the State Council of Aging, and on numerous boards. I could go on, but you get the picture. These were Matthew 25 people, "Lord,-when-was-it-that-we-saw-you-hungry-or-thirsty-or-a-stranger-or-naked-or-sick-or-in-prison?" people.

On Tuesday of Holy Week, Kathi phoned the church office. The situation was still unclear, but Lynne had been hurt. She asked for prayers from her faith community. (Think about this; Kathi was alerting her immediate family to the unfolding situation, and she instinctively contacted her church at the top of the list.)

Charlie and Lynne had spent that morning as they spent every Tuesday morning—picking up donated day-old baked goods and delivering them to residents at the Lincoln Park Towers, a federally subsidized high-rise senior citizens facility in suburban Detroit. They carried the muffins, cake, cookies, and bread into the facility's common room and waited to visit with the residents. Bread delivery wasn't the definitive goal, however. Conversation was. Relationship was the objective.

As the Higgins talked with residents, an angry man entered the room. Technically, Kenneth Miller was too young even to live in the building, but a history of schizophrenia had won him an exemption and an apartment on the thirteenth floor. Lynne and Charlie couldn't have known it, but earlier a staff member had mediated a confrontation between a female resident and Mr. Miller following the woman's accusation that Miller had offended her with inappropriate language and a "dirty joke."[3] Furious after the confrontation, Miller had disappeared to his apartment. Now, ten minutes later, a maintenance man radioed that he was on his way down, armed and shooting.

Charlie and Lynne couldn't have known any of this. They simply heard the shots as bullets ricocheted, popping left and right. Residents rushed for the exit. Except for Charlie and Lynne. Charlie headed toward a phone to call 911. Lynne went the other way, approaching Miller. Sensing that he was heading toward the facility offices to attack the staff, Lynne pled with him. "Stop," she begged. "You don't want to do this."[4]

No one knows exactly what happened next. We know only that Kenneth Miller turned, stopped, and fired. Lynne fell, dead perhaps even by the time her body collapsed to the floor. Miller also shot his accuser and another resident who just happened to be watering plants, both of whom eventually died, and took the elevator up to the thirteenth story. When he reached his floor, he dragged a rug between the elevator

doors to keep those below from using the elevator and he bar-
ricaded himself in his apartment. Out of his apartment win-
dow he fired his .22 rifle at the police below and at the news
helicopters whirling around the building, which we watched
live on CNN Headline News. Several hours later, the SWAT
team rushed Miller's room only to find him sleeping off the
drugs he had ingested after the shootings. "They made me do
it," Miller said afterward. Clearly disoriented and mentally ill,
he added, "I didn't premeditate anything."[5]

Few people can authentically comprehend the trauma
and stress engulfing the Rito and Higgins families over those
next days. On Thursday evening—Maundy Thursday—while
their congregation served communion and recalled Jesus'
commanding "As I have loved you, you also should love one
another" (John 13.34), Lynne's family welcomed a parade of
mourners at a public viewing at the funeral home. Good Fri-
day, they awoke for yet another viewing, this one lasting all
day, for hundreds of well-wishers. Lincoln Park Presbyterian
Church could not seat all who came to the Saturday funeral.
The district's congressman, John Dingell, a longtime family
friend, eulogized Lynne as an exemplar to the nobility of public service.

Sunday, Kathi and Bill woke up, packed their three boys
into the car, and headed to Easter worship, where they sat with
Charlie in the sanctuary where Kathi would later be ordained
an elder, where the boys would lead worship as youth, where
Bill and Kathi would regularly serve bread and wine to God's
people. This was the church building where both parents
taught church school and helped with the youth group. This
was the community Kathi had reflexively notified the moment
she had received the call that her mother had been wounded.
Who could then have known that one son would later become
an overscheduled doctor and yet, with his family, linchpin his
own congregation's mission to the children of incarcerated

people? Would they have predicted that another son would become a church musician, composing a haunting, powerful piece on gun violence written for a string quartet? Surely no one foresaw that the third son would go to seminary and become a clergyman. Now, the funeral over, they simply took grief's first steps forward. They would celebrate the resurrection in holy and generous community with their congregation.

What happened next has fed me in ways I am still discovering. On Tuesday morning after Easter, Kathi and Bill Rito picked up Kathi's recently widowed father, Charlie Higgins, drove to the local bakery, took delivery of its day-old bread, and shared bread and time with the residents of the Lincoln Park Towers.

Those who have experienced God's generosity will not give death the final word. They know exactly where we find living bread.

AFTERWORD

THROUGHOUT THIS BOOK, I HAVE CONNECTED GRATITUDE WITH generosity.

I completed the manuscript for this book in the Spring of 2022. Late in 2023, I asked the publisher to add this afterword, an unusual request so late in the publishing process. To justify my unorthodox plea, I included a brief letter I had written for my family and friends following an unexpected and life-saving surgery.

Five years ago next month, when I was diagnosed as terminal, I resorted to the lessons I had learned from church members who had received the same news over thirty years. I tried to accept the diagnosis with dignity and grace, and I went home to do what terminal patients do: I went on disability; together with Jaci I wrote my funeral service; we refined my will; and I researched my family's genealogy. Last, I finished a long overdue book, and then, well, I waited to die. It wasn't that I wanted to die, or even that I was ready to die. It is simply that Jaci and I resolved that our prayer would be that no matter what, we would try to be faithful to God. I promised myself and God that I would die with dignity.

We each of us have a switch, installed at birth, that directs our thinking about the future. We are naturally adept at thinking about what's next. What will I be when I grow up? What will my life's work be? Where will I live five years from now? With whom shall I share my days? How shall we raise our children? You understand the concept, naturally.

When you receive a terminal diagnosis, you just as naturally know to flip the future switch off because now your days shall not be spent wondering about the future. Now, your days are about remembering the past and preparing your family for your exit. Five years ago I turned my future switch off.

But waiting to die is like buying front row tickets to Hamilton and arriving early, only you notice that the line never moves. It is mind-numbingly boring. So this spring I left hospice long enough for a battery of tests to determine how quickly my illness was progressing. The answer? At a snail's pace. I realized that at this rate, I could stand in line for another 5 to 8 years. Surely, we thought, there is another answer. Despite having long ago accepted my death, Jaci had nonetheless stayed in touch with the University of California at San Diego Hospital, the leading institution in the United States conducting a life-saving surgery for patients with my illness. Despite having declined us twice already, Jaci prevailed one last time to accept me for the surgery. They called on her birthday to offer us a place in the surgery line.

Two days ago, for the first time in almost six years, I used no supplemental oxygen. Yesterday, for the first time in almost four years, I was able to lie flat on a bed without stoking terror-level anxiety of air starvation. They took a monumental risk on me, and the doctor offered today that our story has inspired the entire team. "You were on hospice for three and a half years," he began, "and now you're walking the halls with a giant smile."

I am Lazarus!

When we took the cannula off, I was actually disoriented. I was like a child born without hearing and just now receiving cochlear implants, hearing sound for the first time. I had become accustomed to oxygen; at fourteen liters of oxygen per minute, it was like having a hair dryer up my nose. Now, I keep reaching for my cannula to readjust it only to find that it is not there. I will require a small amount of oxygen when I walk and when I sleep for a couple of months, but in no time I will be completely free of the oxygen tube, that long, green noose.

I am full to overflowing now, three parts gratitude and two parts confusion. You see, I have turned the future switch back on. It's like entering a dark room where the light switch has long been abandoned to an electrical short and still you instinctively flip the switch, and much to your surprise the light actually works again, and the room is suddenly flooded with pure, white light, and you see the contours of the room you haven't noticed in years. What will I do with the rest of my life? Given my God-breathed insights, what might my faithfulness look like now? How can I ever repay the beautiful sense of gratitude I carry for all of you who have supported us in this long season? Better yet, how will I ever repay Jaci for her steadfastness, for her care, for her persistence? I am the only man I know who can say literally that his wife has saved him three times. And like all authentic grace, she never holds it over my head. It is pure gift.

I will still deal with chronic pain in my legs from an earlier surgery, but I am alive— wondrously, joyously, fully alive. Somewhere, maybe thirty years from now, Jaci and I will sit on the porch, rocking back and forth, remembering my lost years.

One of us will say, "What an adventure we have had."

And the other will reply, "Thanks be to God. Thanks be to God."

If I experienced gratitude while on hospice, you can only imagine the gratitude I feel now!

Years ago I was approached by a street evangelist, saying "Have you been saved?" I replied, "Yes. Two thousand years ago. Now the question is, How will I say thank you?"

I feel like that now. Gifted with these stolen days, now the question is, How will my gratitude make me more generous?

How will yours?

NOTES

Preface

1. For a compact synopsis of current research on generosity; its evolutionary, biological, and development roots; its consequences; the individual, social, and cultural factors that influence it; the limitations and future direction of study; and a full bibliography, see Summer Allen, "The Science of Generosity: White paper prepared for the John Templeton Foundation by the Greater Good Science Center at UC Berkeley," (May 2018), https://www.templeton.org/wp-content/uploads/2018/01/Generosity_White_Paper-FinalJTF.pdf.

2. For a fuller exploration of the word "generosity" and its historic development and use, see Christian Smith, and Hilary Davidson, *The Paradox of Generosity: Giving We Receive, Grasping We Lose* (Oxford University Press, 2014), 3–4.

Chapter 1: The Generosity of God

1. For a brief and very readable discussion of this claim, see Thomas Cahill, *The Gifts of the Jews: How a Tribe of Desert Nomads Changed the Way Everyone Thinks and Feels* (New York: Nan A. Talese/ Anchor Books, 1999), 94–96, 128–29.

2. Walter Brueggemann, "The Liturgy of Abundance, the Myth of Scarcity: Consumerism and Religious Life," *Christian Century* (March 24-31, 1999). Reposted at https://www.religion-online.org /article/the-liturgy-of-abundance-the-myth-of-scarcity.

3. James K. Manley, "Spirit," *The Presbyterian Hymnal* (Louisville, KY: Westminster John Knox Press, 1990), 319.

4. James K. Manley, "Spirit, Spirit of Gentleness," *Glory to God* (Louisville, KY: Westminster John Knox Press, 2013), 291.

5. Huston Smith, *The Religions of Man* (New York: Harper & Row, 1965), 316–17.

6. I am aware of and sensitive to the gender-exclusive and undemocratic nuances of the word kingdom. For want of a perfect replacement, however, and to remain biblically resonant, I reluctantly continue its use.

7. Martin Rinkart, "Now Thank We All Our God," *Glory to God* (Louisville, KY: Westminster John Knox Press, 2013), 643.

8. Corrie ten Boom, with John and Elizabeth Sherrill, *The Hiding Place* (Washington Depot, CT: Chosen Books, 1971), 190.

Chapter 2: Generosity for God

1. See Gen. 28:20–22; Lev. 27:30–32; Num. 18:20-32; Deut. 12:5–11, 14:22–29, 26:12–15; 2 Chr. 31:5–15; Neh. 10:37–38, 12:44, 13:5–12; Amos 4:4; Mal. 3:8–10; Matt. 23:23; Luke 11:42, 18:12; Heb. 7:5–9.

2. Andrew McNair, "Why I Tithe—And So Should You," *Forbes*, April 21, 2014, https://www.forbes.com/sites/learnvest/2014/04 /21/why-i-tithe-and-so-should-you/?sh=2c5df6d177a5.

3. Andrew Carnegie, "The Gospel of Wealth" (New York: Carnegie Foundation of New York, 2017 (first published in 1889)).

4. Biologists reject out of hand the fundamental assumptions of social Darwinism, and Darwin would likely have thought social Darwinism a ridiculous caricature. Psychologist Richard Hernstein and political scientist Charles Murray co-authored *The Bell Curve: Intelligence and Class Structure in American Life* in 1994 (New York: Free Press) and claimed that differences of race and class can be explained by genetic factors. In his *New Yorker* review of the book, Stephen Jay Gould wrote, "I can only conclude that [the book's] success in gaining attention must reflect the depressing temper of our time—a historical moment of unprecedented ungenerosity, when a mood for slashing social programs can be powerfully abetted by an argument that beneficiaries cannot be helped, owing to inborn cognitive limits

expressed by low IQ scores." Stephen Jay Gould, "Curveball," *The New Yorker* (November 28, 1994), 139.

5. N.T. Wright, *Surprised by Scripture: Engaging Contemporary Issues* (New York: HarperOne, 2014), 32.

Chapter 3: Generosity with God

1. Sam Wells, *A Nazareth Manifesto: Being with God* (Malden, MA: John Wiley and Sons, 2015), 3.

2. My understanding of the Trinity is shaped by a remarkable book: Jürgen Moltmann, *The Trinity and the Kingdom of God: The Doctrine of God* (San Francisco: Harper & Row, 1981).

3. Sharon Wertz, "Oseola McCarty donates $150,000 to Southern Miss," Press Release, The University of Southern Mississippi, Office of University Communications, https://freerepublic.com/focus/f-news/2613381/posts.

4. Karl Zinsmeister, "The Ones Who Know How to Save," *Philanthropy Roundtable*, n.d., https://www.philanthropyroundtable.org/magazine/the-ones-who-know-how-to-save/.

5. Zinsmeister, "The Ones Who Know."

6. Rick Bragg, "All She Has, $150,000, is Going to a University," *New York Times*, August 13, 1995, https://www.nytimes.com/1995/08/13/us/all-she-has-150000-is-going-to-a-university.html.

7. Rick Bragg, "Oseola McCarty, a Washerwoman Who Gave All She Had to Help Others, Dies at 91," *The New York Times*, September 28, 1999, https://www.nytimes.com/1999/09/28/us/oseola-mccarty-a-washerwoman-who-gave-all-she-had-to-help-others-dies-at-91.html.

8. Kevin Van Hoozer, *Faith Speaking Understanding: Performing the Drama of Doctrine* (Louisville, KY: Westminster John Knox Press, 2014), xvi.

9. Raley Taliaferro, personal interview, April 17, 2015.

10. Bragg, "All She Has."

11. Stephanie Bullock, "Eulogy: Oseola McCarty," *Time Magazine*, October 11, 1999.

Chapter 5: . . . to Clarify Want Versus Need

1. Evan Comen, "The Size of a Home the Year You Were Born," 24/7 Wall St., May 25, 2016, updated December 20, 2021, https://247wallst.com/special-report/2016/05/25/the-size-of-a

-home-the-year-you-were-born/. See also Victoria Araj, "What Is the Average Square Footage of a House? A Guide to House Size," Rocket Mortgage, June 1, 2022. https://www.rocketmortgage.com /learn/average-square-footage-of-a-house.

2. Maria Gatea, "Average Home Size in the US: New Homes Bigger than 10 Years Ago but Apartments Trail Behind," *Storage Café*, October 2, 2020. https://www.storagecafe.com/blog/average-home -size-in-the-us-new-homes-bigger-than-10-years-ago-but-apartments -trail-behind/.

3. "Median Sales Price of Houses Sold for the United States [MSPUS]," U.S. Census Bureau and U.S. Department of Housing and Urban Development, retrieved from FRED, Federal Reserve Bank of St. Louis; https://fred.stlouisfed.org/series/MSPUS, June 15, 2022, https://fred.stlouisfed.org/series/MSPUS.

4. Elizabeth Mendes, "In U.S., Self-Reported Weight Up Nearly 20 Pounds Since 1990," http://www.gallup.com/poll/150947/Self -Reported-Weight-Nearly-Pounds-1990.aspx.

5. "Americans are the unhappiest they've been in 50 years, poll finds," Associated Press, June 16, 2020, https://www.nbcnews .com/politics/politics-news/americans-are-unhappiest-they-ve-been -50-years-poll-finds-n1231153.

6. Gatea, "Average Home Size."

7. Naomi Bloomberg, "Kris Kristofferson," *Encyclopedia Britannica*, October 17, 2023, https://www.britannica.com/biography /Kris-Kristofferson.

8. John and Sylvia Ronsvalle, *The State of Church Giving through 2000, 12th ed.* (Champaign, IL: empty tomb, inc., 2002), 33.

9. Ronsvalle, *The State of Church Giving.*

10. Christian Smith and Hilary Davidson, *The Paradox of Generosity: Giving We Receive, Grasping We Lose* (New York: Oxford University Press, 2014), 104.

11. See the work of Paul Piff, described, among other places, in Ken Stern, "Why the Rich Don't Give to Charity," *Atlantic Monthly*, April 2013, http://www.theatlantic.com/magazine/archive/2013/04/why -the-rich-dont-give/309254/, and Lisa Miller, "The Money-Empathy Gap," *New York Magazine*, July 1, 2012, http://nymag.com/news /features/money-brain-2012-7/.

Chapter 7: . . . to Dethrone the Chief Idols of the Age

1. This saying is an adaptation first made popular by Arthur G. Gish, *Beyond the Rat Race* (Scottdale, PA: Herald Press, 1973), 21.

2. A. Scott Berg, *Wilson* (New York: G.P. Putnam's Sons, 2013), 87.

3. Richard Foster, *Celebration of Discipline: The Path to Spiritual Growth*, rev. ed. (San Francisco: Harper & Row, 1988), 80.

Chapter 8: . . . to Serve as Spiritual Discipline

1. Refers to the influential book by Tom Friedman, *The World is Flat: A Brief History of the 21st Century* (New York: Farrar, Straus and Giroux, 2005).

2. Phyllis Tickle lectured broadly and wrote extensively about the emergent church, and I have found her thought-provoking and helpful. The reference to a "five-hundred-year garage sale" comes from *The Great Emergence: How Christianity Is Changing and Why* (Grand Rapids: Baker, 2008).

Chapter 10: The Pastor's Internal Dialogue

1. Gregory A. Smith, "About Three-in-Ten U.S. Adults Are Now Religiously Unaffiliated," December 14, 2021, Pew Research Center, https://www.pewresearch.org/religion/2021/12/14/about-three-in-ten-u-s-adults-are-now-religiously-unaffiliated/.

2. "Meet the 'Spiritual but Not Religious,'" April 6, 2017, Barna, https://www.barna.com/research/meet-spiritual-not-religious/.

Chapter 11: The Pastor Speaks with Congregation Leaders

1. Rick Jones, "Congregations Are in Decline, but Age Remains the Same," Presbyterian Church (USA), Office of the General Assembly, March 1, 2019, https://www.pcusa.org/news/2019/3/1/congregations-are-decline-age-ranges-remain-same/.

2. Yonat Shimron, "Study: Attendance Hemorrhaging at Small and Midsize US Congregations," Religious News Service, October 14, 2021, https://religionnews.com/2021/10/14/study-attendance-at-small-and-midsize-us-congregations-is-hemorrhaging/.

3. Christian Smith and Hilary Davidson, *The Paradox of Generosity: Giving We Receive, Grasping We Lose* (New York: Oxford University Press, 2014), 13.

4. Frederick Buechner, *Whistling in the Dark: An ABC Theologized* (San Francisco: Harper & Row, 1988), 74.

5. David Leonhardt, "What Makes People Give?" *New York Times*, March 9, 2008, http://www.nytimes.com/2008/03/09/magazine/09Psychology-t.html?pagewanted=1.

Conclusion

1. Anne Lamott, *Traveling Mercies: Some Thoughts on Faith* (New York: Pantheon, 1999), 131.

2. *The Book of Order 2019-2021*, Presbyterian Church (USA) (Louisville, KY: Presbyterian Publishing Corporation, 2019), 2.

3. David Goodman, "Michigan Shooting Suspect Arrested," AP News, April 19, 2000, https://apnews.com/article/7a4ca195008f33 a0ecc005d53e320a0a.

4. Interview with Kathi Rito, April 22, 2022.

5. "Hearing Postponed for Michigan Shooter," UPI Archives, April 21, 2000, https://www.upi.com/Archives/2000/04/21/Hearing -postponed-for-Michigan-shooter/7876956289600/.

Printed in the USA
CPSIA information can be obtained
at www.ICGtesting.com
CBHW072030150724
11533CB00002B/2